eBay®
Online Auctions

D0878465

This book is not authorized, sponsored by, or affiliated with eBay Inc.

By Neil J. Salkind with Bruce Frey

e-Bay® Online Auctions:
Effective Buying and Selling with e-Bay®

Library of Congress Catalog Card Number: 99-62264

ISBN: 0-9662889-4-7

5   4   3   2   1

Educational facilities, companies, and organizations interested in multiple copies of this book should contact the publisher for quantity discount information. Training manuals, CD-ROMs, electronic versions, and portions of this book are also available individually or can be tailored for specific needs.

MUSKA&LIPMAN

Muska & Lipman Publishing
9525 Kenwood Road, Suite 16-372
Cincinnati, Ohio 45242
www.muskalipman.com
publisher@muskalipman.com

This book is composed in Glasgow, Helvetica, and Courier typefaces
using QuarkXpress 4.0.4, Adobe PhotoShop 5.0, and Adobe Illustrator 8.0.
Printed in Cincinnati, Ohio in the United States of America

http://www.muskalipman.com

Credits

Publishing Manager
Andy Shafran

Editorial Services Manager
Elizabeth A. Bruns

Development Editor
Ben Milstead

Copy Editor
Tonya Maddox

Technical Editor
J. Eric Slone

Proofreader
Audrey Grant

Cover Designer
Dave Abney

Production Manager
Cathie Tibbetts

Production Team
DOV Graphics
    Dave Abney
    Stephanie Archbold
    Michelle Frey
    Linda Worthington

Indexer
Cary Sherman

Printer
C.J. Krehbiel Co.

http://www.muskalipman.com

About the Author

Neil J. Salkind has been writing trade books for about ten years and among his credits are *The Big Mac Book, Running Works for Windows, Windows Illustrated* and *The Online Epicure*. He is the only writer to have won two Computer Press Association awards for introductory computer books. In his spare time, he teaches child development at the University of Kansas in Lawrence. For fun, he writes the nationally published *Online Epicure* food column, swims, cooks, reads and collects signed first editions of books.

Acknowledgements

A book is far more than words on pages—and this book was created and produced by far more people than just the authors. In this spirit, we would like to thank Andy Shafran for his foresight, hard work and good humor to ensure that this book came to fruition. All publishers should be as attentive to their writers as Andy.

I'd also like to thank Elizabeth Bruns, editorial services manager at Muska & Lipman, who saw to it that the various drafts went where they should when they should and oversaw the entire quality control process. Thanks also go out to Ben Milstead and his colleagues who developed and edited the text to make it more readable, but also approachable. Finally, thanks to DOV Graphics, who saw to it that everything came together to be the book that it is.

—Neil J. Salkind

Table of Contents

Table of Contents

Table of Contents

Table of Contents

of Contents

Table of Contents

Table of Contents

Table of Contents

Table of Contents

Table of Contents

of Contents

Table of Contents

Feedback: Knowing Who You're Dealing With 84

Section 3 Selling

Going, Going, Gone!

Going, Going, Gone!

Going, Going, Gone!

Going, Going, Gone

oing, Gone!

Introduction
Going, Going, Gone!

Going, Going, Gone!

Going, Going, Gone!

Going, Going, Gone!

Going, Going, Gone

oing, Gone!

Introduction
Going, Going, Gone!

What an idea! I need that baseball card of yours to complete my collection and you're willing to sell it for the right price. After a little bit of back and forth between the two of us, I agree to meet your price. I send you payment, you send me my newly purchased find—and we're both happy as clams.

That's the way many traditional purchases work, but these days things are a bit different. From your cozy living room in Vermont in your pajamas or on your laptop in your hotel room near Trafalgar Square in London, you can buy and sell through eBay (**www.ebay.com**), the first hugely successful online auction service.

How successful is it? Take a look at these numbers:

▶ As of this writing, there are almost 2 million items for sale on eBay and almost 50 million have already been sold.

▶ More than 175 million bids have been entered at a rate of about 120,000 bids per day. That's a lot of Beanie Babies.

▶ There are more than 500,000 registered users just like you. They're looking to add to their favorite collection of Tiffin glass vases or to start a full-time business selling rare books on eBay.

▶ The last quarter of 1998 saw more than $55 million in merchandise sales.

▶ Every 24 hours some 200,000 items are added to the list.

▶ And eBay's home page is viewed more than 600 million times each month.

That's a lot of auctioneering.

Who had this terrific idea? Pierre Omidyar, former computer programmer, Web page designer, and the creator of eBay.

Pierre's friend collected Pez dispensers. She asked Pierre why there was not an easier way to buy and sell them on the Internet; she wanted to easily manage her personal collection. Doing what he did best, Pierre started a simple Web page in 1995 and lived the dream of all entrepreneurs: He couldn't open all the mail that arrived. With the vision for what electronic commerce (or e-commerce) could be, eBay was born. Buyers and sellers everywhere have embraced without reservation.

For example, Ben Wilson paid for graduate school by selling his 30-year-old comic collection on eBay. Bill Yost used to be a chemist—now he buys and sells Tiffin glass as a full-time business out of his home in Florence, KY. Linda Margolin (who has a fun eBay user ID of Moon) is a freelance photographer who displays and sells her photos on eBay—enough to purchase the new equipment she needs for her business. Is this great, or what?

If you're a shopper or seller (and who among us is not?) and just a little adventurous, then the eBay online auction service and *eBay Online Auctions* is just for you. In *eBay Online Auctions*, we will walk you through every single operation you need to get started buying and selling items of your choice. We'll show you how to contact sellers to tell them what a satisfied customer you are (or aren't), how to run an auction that gets the best prices possible, and how to find such treasures as a 1964 soundtrack of "A Hard Day's Night."

We'll do all these things in a way that is easy and informative, via the most often asked questions. This way, you can go directly to the questions you need an answer to or read through questions in a specific area to find out all about how a particular component of eBay works.

And, we'll provide all this information to you in a special format using question and answer format. We think that listing the most common questions that new and experienced eBay users might ask, and then answering them is the best way to learn how to use eBay. In addition, there are other features that you will find throughout the book, such as personal anecdotes from eBay users, that help show you how eBay can be used (and misused!). We also include brief discussions about special ways that eBay can be used and introduce new terms by printing them in **bold**. We also **bold URLs** so you can refer back to them readily. You'll find a definition of all these terms in the Glossary at the end of *eBay Online Auctions.*

Ready to have some fun? Fire up your computer and get on this e-commerce rocket to the future and let's get started.

Getting Started

Getting Started

Getting Started

Getting Started

ting Started

Section 1
Getting Started

Getting Started

Getting Started

Getting Started

Getting Started

Getting Started

1
Getting Started

Let's be honest: eBay is the most fun you can have and still be legal. If you like shopping, eBay is for you. If you like computers, eBay is for you. If you like to shop using your computer, you're in the good company of tens of thousands of people who use eBay each day to buy and sell their treasures.

Whether you're an experienced eBayer or not, there's important information in this section of *eBay Online Auctions* that will help you get the most out of eBay.

We start with a discussion of the basics, including what eBay is, how it works, and how to find it on the Internet. We review the contents of the home page and then discuss how eBay helps ensure the safety of all transactions. Finally, we introduce you to eBay etiquette—what's nice and what's not when buying and selling—and then talk about customizing eBay for your personal use.

Our travels lead you to see what's biddable on eBay, with ideas for what you might want to sell as well. Like any group of people who are interested in similar activities (such as collecting) you'll learn about the eBay community. This community is very much alive, with members constantly talking to one another about what they have to buy and sell and more—the personal side of having a passion and wanting to share it.

Need help? It's on eBay in many different formats, available at the click of a mouse. If you can't find an answer to your question—don't forget to look in *eBay Online Auctions* or try eBay's live help feature, available 24 hours a day. We'll end the first part of *eBay Online Auctions* with a description of how the service can personalize your membership and activity through its *About Me* feature. And finally, you'll learn exactly how to become a registered user—your first step in joining the most revolutionary and exciting Internet commerce idea to ever come along.

Say Hello to eBay

Q1 What is eBay and how does it work?

eBay is the first and most successful online auction that allows buying and selling over the Internet. Each day it offers millions of items that are bought and sold by people just like you. Whether you have a restored 1983 Mustang convertible to sell or are looking for a rare "My Little Pony," eBay is for you.

eBay has several advantages over a traditional auction. Because it is on the Internet, it is easily accessible and millions of people can participate at the same time; there are thousands of items to consider across hundreds of categories. Now that eBay has gone global (See **Question 56**), there are no geographical boundaries. Best of all, you set the price that you want to pay and in the free market's wisdom, the best price wins. Everyone has an equal and independent chance of being the highest bidder. You can be involved in one auction or 100 auctions all at the same time and eBay tells you the moment you have been outbid by another bidder.

eBay is also like a traditional auction in many ways. You find what you like, make a bid, and then wait for others to bid. If you are outbid, you can raise your bid or drop out of the auction. The highest bidder wins and takes home the turkey (or 1980 Silver Shadow Rolls Royce with a current bid of $21,800 as the case might be).

How does eBay work? Here are the basic steps for buying and selling. In each case you need to first register with eBay (See **Question 14**).

If you're buying:

1. Search on eBay until you find the item you want to buy.

2. Place a bid.

3. Check your email so you know your status as a bidder in the auction.

4. Once the item is yours (if you win the auction), you'll get an email from eBay notifying you. You can then make arrangements with the seller for payment. Payment is most often made using a money order or a cashier's or bank check.

If you're selling:

1. Create an auction listing describing the item(s) you want to sell.

2. Participate in your auction by promptly answering any inquiries from bidders.

3. Once the item is sold, make arrangements with the high bidder for payment.

Make sure to pay eBay for their services. The cost is based on the item's final price (in addition to a base cost for listing an item). This really isn't rocket science. In fact, as you learn about one facet of eBay while reading through this book, you'll see that the others become clearer and easier to use as well.

Q2 I'll take a look. Where can I find eBay?

It is on the Internet at **http://www.ebay.com** and you get there by entering this URL (Uniform Resource Locator) in the location line of your Internet browser and pressing the Enter key.

Know what a URL is? It's the address of a particular Web page. With most modern Web browsers and for most Web addresses, you need not enter the http:// (known as a **protocol handler**). In addition, for the newest versions of Netscape Navigator and Microsoft Internet Explorer (in their default configurations), all you need to enter are the letters that spell eBay.

You can't call or write eBay to make a bid. The Internet is the only way you can participate.

With popular Internet sites such as eBay, you might find that there is so much Web traffic, it may be difficult to make a connection. This is especially true around holidays such as Christmas and Valentine's Day. Be patient; the eBay people are constantly adding more capacity to their system. In the meantime, go inventory your collection of buffalo nickels and get ready to sell the whole herd!

Q3 eBay is only available on the Internet and I'm not an Internet expert. Are you sure I can participate?

Absolutely. You need very few Internet skills to use eBay and you can develop those skills as you go along. Practice makes perfect and familiarity with eBay will build your confidence as well as your buying and selling skills.

Something you must have is a connection to the Internet. Explaining how to hook-up to the Internet goes beyond the scope of this book, but you can call a local Internet Service Provider, speak with the computer guru at work or at your children's school (all kids already know how to do this stuff, right?), or talk with the people who sold you your computer to get on the Internet. A good book that can help is *Sams Teach Yourself the Internet in 10 Minutes, Second Edition* by Galen Grimes (ISBN 0672316102).

Here are the basic skills you need in order to navigate and use eBay successfully:

▶ Use simple words when you search for an item or enter a bid.

▶ Click and double-click your mouse.

▶ Know the basics of navigating on the World Wide Web including clicking on links, moving to the next and previous pages, and printing out pages.

These three skills can be learned from any one of many introductory trade books on the market or from simple tutorials that came along with your computer. Using eBay is easier (and more fun) than using a word processor or spreadsheet or any other application you might own. You'll be participating like a pro in this online auction in no time at all.

Trading with eBay

"I started out selling Mexican Coca-Cola and Pepsi items and did well. If I got an overseas bidder, I would email the bidder and we would work out a trade where I would have them go to their local store and get me some Coke or Pepsi (cans or bottles). Now I have over 300 foreign cans and bottles and my collection is getting bigger every day! Thanks to eBay!"

—Steve from Oregon

Q4 Wow, this home page is loaded. What's all that stuff?

It certainly is loaded. You can see where everything starts—eBay's home page—in **Figure 1.1**. Let's go through and identify some of eBay's most important home page features.

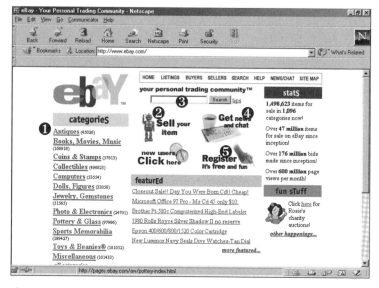

❶ Click on any one of these category names to see items for sale on eBay.

❷ Click here to sell an item.

❸ Enter a search term here and click the button labeled Search to find a particular item on eBay.

❹ Click here to find out the latest about eBay.

❺ Click here to register on eBay and start selling or bidding.

Figure 1.1 eBay's home page is colorful and inviting and just shouts for you to start bidding or selling.

From the top, first, there's the colorful eBay symbol. To the immediate right of the symbol, you'll find eight links you see here:

| HOME | LISTINGS | BUYERS | SELLERS | SEARCH | HELP | NEWS/CHAT | SITE MAP |

These links take you to special eBay places, all of which provide a specific type of information and additional links to other eBay sites as well. These eight links are available on every eBay page, so they are always accessible.

▶ Home takes you back to the home page, which you see in Figure 1.1.

▶ Listings shows you what's available in the Featured Auctions and Hot Items areas of eBay (See **Question 26**). These are special listings you'll learn about later in this book. Listings also contains all the eBay categories into which items can be placed for buying and selling.

▶ Buyers takes you to eBay Buyers Services, where you can get initial information on bidding and buying items that appear on eBay (See **Question 43**).

▶ Sellers takes you to Seller Services, which has information about setting up auctions and selling on eBay (See **Question 57**).

▶ The Search link allows you to see if an item is available on eBay. You can search with the object's name, who bid on it, who is selling it, and the country the item is located. eBay also uses a very powerful search engine that lets you perform intricate and precise searches. If it's there, you'll find it (See **Question 29**).

▶ Help gives you instructions on how to perform common eBay tasks. It's the place to turn to if you have a question for which you cannot find the answer. There's even live, interactive help staffed by real people! See **Question 23** for information about Help.

▶ News/Chat (See **Question 24**) takes you to the latest and greatest happenings in the eBay community. It also leads you to discussion or chat groups on any of the major eBay categories, including coins, dolls, comics, and pottery.

▶ The site map gives you the overall tour of just what's on eBay's Web site and how you can easily get there. This is a terrific place to visit and discover some of the less obvious (but just as important) features that eBay offers. It's also a great place to start your eBay session, since anything new shows up here; this is often the only eBay place that can take you directly to any other eBay pages.

Want to get started searching for items right away? There is a Search box just underneath the main links and the "your personal trading community" eBay statement. The Search icon, shown here, is what you click to find what you are looking for:

Search

Click the Search button after filling in the information and wait for eBay to find the closest match to the terms you entered. We'll show you how to search effectively and efficiently, beginning with **Question 29**.

The real action starts along the left side of the page, where the various eBay categories are listed. We'll describe each category starting with **Question 9**, but just a quick look gives you some idea of the scope of what's available on eBay.

Those little numbers to the right of each category? They are the number of items currently available in any one category. For the opening Web page you see in Figure 1.1, the number of collectibles (in the many different subcategories) is 496,823. Looking at all those would surely keep you busy. Maybe that's why the average eBay user spends more than two hours at the site during any one visit! One click on any one category takes you to a listing of all the items in that category or to subcategories.

To the right of the category list and under the Search box are eBay icons and accompanying descriptions:

▶ Click Sell Your Item when you are ready to start selling.

▶ Click Get News and Chat when you want the latest on eBay or want to talk with other eBay users.

▶ Click New Users Click Here if you want an introduction to eBay and what it offers.

▶ Click Register—It's free and fun, to start the registration process

These icons generally help get you started with everything from getting ready to sell to what to do if you're new. You'll find the featured auctions mentioned earlier under featured. This is the same list of items you get when you click on the Listings icon at the top of the eBay home page. You can see more featured items for sale by clicking the more featured link at the bottom of the screen.

Let's move on. The right side of the opening home page holds some interesting statistics about eBay's growth. Beneath that is eBay's Fun Stuff area, a collection of what's going on these days at eBay!

That's the eBay home page in a nutshell. If you intend to do lots of eBay stuff, why not make this your default home page so that every time you open your Internet browser, you'll go to eBay? Different browsers allow you to do this in different ways, so check the Help option and find out how to do it on yours.

Does anyone know really what time it is?

When you start bidding, you have to know what time it is in eBayland in order to accurately estimate how much time is left in an auction. You can see the cool eBay time map of the United States by clicking the Listings link at the top of the home page and then clicking *Check eBay official time.*

You'll see a nice map with the time zones and corresponding times (**Figure 1.2**). If you're bidding from the East coast and you see that an eBay auction ends at 10 p.m., it may be 10 p.m. West coast time—but it's 1 A.M. (yawn) your time. Maybe you can find an alarm clock on eBay to wake you up for that last bid?

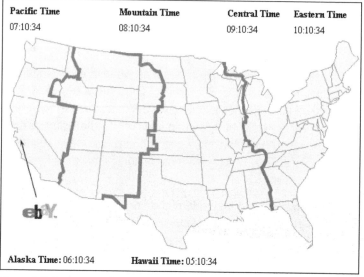

Pacific Time	Mountain Time	Central Time	Eastern Time
07:10:34	08:10:34	09:10:34	10:10:34

Alaska Time: 06:10:34   **Hawaii Time:** 05:10:34

Figure 1.2 Be sure you know what time it is since it is always Pacific Time as far as eBay is concerned.

Q5

I'm a little more comfortable with this eBay home page, but how will I ever know all that's available on eBay and learn to get around?

You will find every feature that eBay provides on the site map, which is accessible from the eBay page shown in Figure 1.1. Just click on the site map link and you will see (**Figure 1.3**) eBay's complete organization, including what features you can reach with one click of the mouse.

Home Listings Buyers Sellers Search Help News/Chat Site Map

Try a new way to shop - browse Antique listings by photos.
What's new about Feedback Forum? Check it out!

eBay Site Map

Section 1 Getting Started

Welcome
Tutorial
    Registration
    Finding Stuff
    Bidding
    Proxy Bidding Example
    Selling
Go Global! NEW!
Community Center NEW!
eBay Life NEW!
The eBay Store

Quick Links

Current Listings
Gallery NEW!
Big Ticket items
Featured Auctions
New Today
Ending Today
Completed Auctions
eBay Categories
eBay Category Overview
Going, going, gone
Search
    Search Tips

Buyer Services
General Buyer Information
    About Me NEW!
    Helpful Services NEW!
    Registered User Information
    Buyer Tips
    After the Auction Tips
    Gift Section NEW!
Bidding Management
    My eBay
    Retract a Bid
    Wanted Page

Seller Services
General Seller Information
    About Me NEW!
    Helpful Services NEW!
    Registered User Information
    Seller Tips
    After the Auction Tips
    Link Buttons NEW!
    Gift Icon NEW!
Item Management
    My eBay
    Add Item
    Quick Add Item
    Add to Item Description
    Feature an Auction
    Change Item Category
    Retrieve Your Listings Summary
    End Auction Early
    Cancel a Bid
    Relist Item
Billing Information
    Account Status
    eBay Fees
    Payment Coupon
    Payment Terms
    Place or Update your Credit Card
    Submitting credit card information to eBay
    Final Value Fee Credit Request
    Account Refunds
    Automatic Auction Extension

Registered User Services
General Information
    About Me NEW!
    Register
    Contact Other Registered User
    Change Registered Information
    Change Notification Preferences NEW!
Account Information
    Account Status
User ID and E-mail Information
    Change User ID
    Change E-mail Address
    Request A Person's User ID History
    Request Another Person's E-mail Address
    Request Multiple Persons' E-mail Addresses
Password Services
    Confirm New Registration
    Confirm Change E-mail Address
    Forgot Password
    Change Password
Feedback
    Feedback Forum
    Leave Feedback
    View Feedback
    Complaints about Other Users
Transaction Management
    After the Auction

Information
Guidelines
FAQ
User ID FAQ
Privacy Policy
Revised User Agreement NEW!
User Agreement Revision FAQ NEW!
Contact eBay
Legal Buddy Program NEW!
DMCA Registered Agent
Piracy FAQ NEW!

eBay Bulletin Boards
eBay Cafe
eBay Cafe for AOL Users
Announcements
Wanted Board
Q & A Board
Support Q & A Board
Support Q & A Board for New Users
Help with Images and HTML

Figure 1.3 The site map is eBay central control—from here, you can get to anywhere (on eBay, that is).

In fact, the site map will be the main tool you use to get to different parts of eBay. For example, want to go to *eBay Life,* the eBay community newsletter? The site map beckons for your clicks!

The site map is the place to go if you need to find information about both the regular eBay features (such as listing and feedback information) and new features.

Experienced eBayers make the site map their first stop when they start a new eBay session just to see what new information or features might be offered. A new feature is indicated by the *New* graphic to the right of any new entry on eBay. Here's an example:

About Me NEW!

eBay uses lots of cool little icons and images to help visually communicate what's happening at the site. In particular, any feature that is new is usually accompanied by the new icon to the right of the site map location. Just a quick glance over the site map every few days should tell you what's new; just a click takes you there.

Q6 I know it's early to ask, but this payment thing bothers me. Sending money to someone I don't know and giving out my credit card number make me nervous. What kind of security safeguards are there?

Your hesitation about sending money (be it a check or otherwise) or giving out your credit card number is understandable. Everyone is anxious about such transactions at first, but when you see how eBay works and learn that your accounts can be kept safe and you can take steps to help ensure that, you'll have more confidence in the system.

If you're a buyer, you usually have the option to pay by personal check or money order, which you can purchase at the post office or bank; you can sometimes use a credit card. The seller will probably want your personal check to clear (which can take up to 10 days but usually takes only a few) before sending the merchandise to you. If you need something in a hurry, pay for it via money order. A money order costs about $1.00. Never, never, ever, cross-your-heart-and-hope-to-die, send cash. That's an invitation to disaster.

If you're a seller, you'll pay eBay a commission via credit card. eBay uses the latest technology to ensure that credit card numbers are kept secret and secure.

If you want to go the extra step, you can use escrow services which adds an additional fee (See **Question 55**) and where a private company acts as a go-between to ensure that the buyer sends his or her money and the seller's item is as described during the auction.

What are some of the rules I need to know as an eBay user?

Just like any community, the whole enterprise falls apart if rules aren't well-defined and followed. If Joe promises (by being high bidder) to purchase those antique marbles from Betty and then doesn't come through, that leaves the rest of us in doubt. Will the whole system work? It works because Joe and Betty have stipulated, through the terms of the **user agreement**, to fulfill their obligations. There are some major rules that eBay wants you to follow and others you should consider just because it makes good sense to be a good online eBayer.

eBay Etiquette

Directly from the eBay Community Guidelines page, eBay etiquette is:

▶ We believe people are basically good.

▶ We believe everyone has something to contribute.

▶ We believe that an honest, open environment can bring out the best in people.

▶ We recognize and respect everyone as a unique individual.

▶ We encourage you to treat others the way that you want to be treated.

These are self-explanatory. If you can't abide by these easy rules, maybe it's time to start your own electronic auction. No one who participates in the eBay community wants to be a stickler about the way members behave, but there must be an understanding between participants in order for things to run smoothly. While the five beliefs certainly sound appropriate, the following section describes five of our own.

> *"On February 1st my dogs got out of my back yard and when I got a call at work, I went home to find them. They ended up playing down the street from the house and were out for about an hour when I found [one dog] Dusty on the corner. He looked fine when he walked up and jumped in the car but then he started acting funny. I took him to the vet where I found out he had been shot twice. We had no idea where Zoe, our other dog, was. We had the local paper do a story and three days later, sadly, she was found dead, four miles out of town with a bullet in the back.*
>
> *To save Dusty, it was going to be a great deal of money and I sent emails to my friends on eBay and soon we were receiving money donations, of around $400, to help with the bill. Without all the eBayers, we would be in a great deal of trouble. That's my story about the nice folks on eBay!"*
>
> *–Susan from Toledo*

eBay Online Auctions Etiquette

Here's a set of guidelines we've come up with to make your experience on eBay as smooth as possible.

▶ **Don't bid on an item unless you're serious about buying it.**

It's always fun to bid and see your name on the eBay screen, but unless you are really interested in an item, don't waste your time or the time of the seller who reviews bids. Other bidders also watch the item as the price increases and base their own actions on recent bids.

▶ **Propose what you think is a fair price as your bid.**

For the most part, the seller and the type of auction take care of bids that are too low, but the whole idea of a community of buyers and sellers works better if fair prices are the target. That way, the seller makes a little money and can afford to sell again and the buyer keeps the standards of the buying in the community where they belong—high.

▶ **Don't misrepresent what you sell in its value, price, or description.**

There's nothing worse and more potentially destructive to any online activity, let alone one where money changes hands, than when people (such as sellers) misrepresent themselves and what it is they are trying to sell. It sours everyone and endangers the whole system. If that cobalt blue, heart-shaped perfume bottle has a slight chip, mention that in the description; then it will be more understandable why the price is so low. If the sterling Tiffany perfume bottle is flawless, mention that as well; that way the buyer knows why the asking price is so high. Such details may actually increase the likelihood of selling because now buyers trust you a little more.

▶ **Don't use eBay for your own commercial gain at the expense of the eBay community.**

Unscrupulous people may go to an eBay auction, get an email address, and then offer to the bidder the same item for much less then the seller is asking—all outside an auction. This practice is called **siphoning** and it's certainly inconsistent with the goals and guidelines offered by eBay.

▶ **When you buy, send your payment promptly. When you sell, send your item as soon as payment is received and accepted.**

Package it securely to ensure that it gets where it's going still looking the way you described it. We need not say much more about this, except that the faster everyone gets what they want, the faster the bidding and selling can begin again! Andále! Andále!

 Any other general things to remember about using eBay?

You asked for it. Here are our 10 commandments for shopping eBay (or any other online auction). While these are not as important as the original set that was carved in stone, it is a good idea to at least read and consider these. We'll be coming back to some of these in later sections of the book.

Commandment #1: *Do your homework.*

Find out as much as you can about the auction site (which in our case is eBay) and how it works. Read about the site (given the information that the site itself provides), but also search the Internet for other comments and relevant information.

Commandment #2: *If you're ready to buy, know what you're looking for.*

For example, if you are looking for a laptop computer, have some idea what features you are interested in. It won't hurt to change your shopping list once you get started, but it's useful to have a general idea of what you want when you set out.

Commandment #3: *Consider hidden costs.*

There are always costs associated with an auction that you may not immediately see. For example, if you are the winning bidder on an item, you usually have to pay shipping. Do you have to pay insurance as well? Are shipping and insurance combined in one cost? Know what you're paying for.

Commandment #4: *Monitor your use.*

It's not common, but people can become addicted to online auctions such that it becomes the focal point for all their activities. If it's no longer business or no longer fun, it's time for help.

Commandment #5: *If you're selling, check out the buyer; if you're buying, check out the seller.*

Most auction sites, eBay in particular, have extensive feedback systems for and about both buyers and sellers. If you're ever suspicious, don't sell to a particular person or buy from a particular person.

Commandment #6: *Plan ahead.*

An online auction isn't the place to order that first edition your honey wants yesterday. First, you have to be the high bidder, and then you have to wait until the auction is over to claim your prize. Then it has to be mailed or shipped to you! This all takes time and if you're a smart online auction participant, allow at least two weeks for everything. (On eBay, even the longest normal auction only lasts 7 days but during holidays, an auction can run for 14 days.)

Commandment #7: *Say what you mean and mean what you say.*

If you're a buyer, your bid and your words (email to the seller) are taken at full value. You are usually welcome to ask all the questions via email you want. Be sure you ask what you want to know so there will be no surprises. If you're a seller, be very sure that you have clearly described what it is you are selling in words and (if you include them) pictures. A major complaint that buyers have after the sale is that the item did not meet their expectations—which usually means it was not as described.

Commandment #8: *Know how much you can afford to spend.*

Many experienced eBayers think that the first rule of buying via an auction is to set an upper limit for an item and not go beyond that. It's too easy to get caught up and bid beyond what you can afford (and what the item is worth). Keep in mind that almost every type of item imaginable will be offered again someday and maybe at a price you can afford.

Commandment #9: *If it's too good to be true...*

You've heard this one before from your mother! She was right. If you see an X-men #94 comic in mint condition for $20.00, the auction is over in a few minutes—and you know it's worth $350—it's either not in mint condition or something weird is happening. The answer? Use common sense.

Commandment #10: *Pay in a way that allows you some recourse.*

This usually means using a credit card. If justified, you can always charge it back to the sponsoring bank. More and more online sellers are offering credit card payment. Never pay in cash or at least not in your own country. Some foreign buyers have no other way than to pay in their own currency, but be sure to check exchange rates and such. A seller's request to pay in cash can be a warning sign that things are not right. If the item is costly enough, use an escrow agent to act in the transaction. There's more about escrow services in **Question 55**.

Seeing What's on eBay

What are some of the things I can purchase on eBay?

Time for some fun.

At first, eBay had only one category (Pez dispensers, remember?). Then it had a few categories; then a couple of hundred; and now more than a thousand, with additional ones being added every day.

The fastest way to find out what categories eBay offers is to go to the eBay Category Overview (**Figure 1.4**). You can easily reach it from the site map. This is a complete listing of all categories, plus all levels within each category.

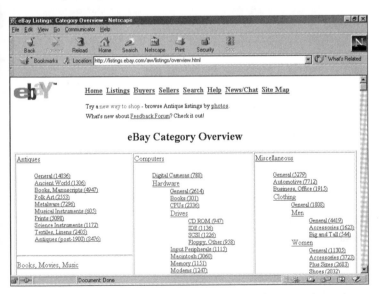

Figure 1.4 Click on any one of these categories to see the current items that are up for auction.

If you click on the category on the eBay home page, you're sent to an abbreviated listing that contains just the main and first level categories.

Categories have main headings (such as Antiques) and subheadings (such as General or Ancient World). You should also notice that each subcategory is accompanied by a small number (for instance, the 14036 next to the General subcategory under Antiques in Figure 1.4). This number indicates the number of items that are available for auction in that category. As you might expect, these numbers change throughout the day.

Here's a listing of the 12 categories available as of this writing. We're also showing you some of the subcategories so you can get a feeling for what's there.

Categories change, they are deleted and replaced, so it's a good idea to check the eBay Category Overview page often to see what's available at any time.

▶ Antiques. Cool old stuff such as books and manuscripts, folk art, prints and scientific instruments. What's for sale today? Take a look at three different items up for auction:

—A 1865 rare Abraham Lincoln book for $12.00

—A Wallace Nutting print for $9.99

—A copper incubator/beautiful/rare for $350.00

▶ Books, Movies, Music. *The Old Man and the Sea*, "Broadway", Guns & Roses? This huge category covers everything from rare books to magazines about pets to CDs and records. Some recent offerings:

—Tarzan, Princess Of Mars $52.00

—*Life* 1972 Diana Ross $15.00

—Two Peter, Paul & Mary 45s $3.00

▶ Coins and Stamps. Who would have thought that there would be almost 2,000 items available in the Exonumia subcategory? Not us. In fact, we didn't even know what it was until we took a look and found the category full of medals and tokens. Other coin and stamp stuff includes U.S. and non-U.S., including all the supplies you'd need for these pursuits. Here are some of the spare change and stamps available:

—Quarters—64 different—1844-1930 $190.00

—524 Green $5.00 Vf+ $5.00

—Australia: Four Bird FDC's $3.00

▶ Collectibles. This is an amazingly huge category, including everything from Barbie dolls to advertising signs to comic books to fishing lures to pictures of "the king" (Elvis, that is). This category is really one of eBay's "black holes," where passionate collectors come and stay for hours at a time. Some recent treasures include the following:

—Elvis "Frankie And Johnny" Mono RCA LPM-3553 $1.00

—1958 Walter Lantz Charlie/Homer $24.99

—Kansas City Fire Department Uniform T-Shirt $15.00

▶ Computers. The items offered here turn over as fast as the technology is developing, but you can find everything from inexpensive tape drives to discontinued Apple eMates.

—New Avatar Shark 250mb Mobile Hard Drive $61.01

—New Digital Camera! Put Photos on eBay! $89.00

—CorelDraw 8 Full Version Retail Box $96.95

▶ Dolls and Figures. Madame Alexander, Raggedy Ann, G.I. Joe, and even Ginny Dolls. What more could you ask for? Here's a sampling:

—Mattel 1970 Little Miss Cheerleader O.U. $10.00

—Mint In Box 1963 Skipper ~ Mattel $20.00

—Original Xavier Roberts Cabbage Patch Doll $150.00

▶ Jewelry and Gemstones. Costume, carved, and contemporary—jewelry to match any taste and pocket book. There are beads, watches, and other elegant items:
   —Baby Swiss Blue Topaz 15ct Parcel $15.50
   —Art Nouveau Fly/Jewel Belt Buckle $7.50
   —Statue Of Liberty Pin $1.99

▶ Photo and Electronics. You can find plenty of the general consumer electronics (stereos, personal tape players, and so on) and even a satellite dish or two, one for your city and one for your country home:
   —New Dish Network System 9.95 W/ Install Video $9.95
   —Harman Kardon Avr20 Surround Receiver $189.00
   —Watson 100 Bulk Film Loader (35mm) Like New $1.00

▶ Pottery and Glass. Remember the sign in the store: If you break it, you bought it?" No danger of that here; just beautiful pictures of beautiful objects. Here's a plate full of glass, pottery, and porcelain:
   —Tiffin Crystal Pheasant Paperweight $50.00
   —Regal Old McDonald Butter Dish $49.95
   —Fire King Black Dot Bowl $15.00

▶ Sports Memorabilia. Believe it or not, the auction for the $3,000,000 price paid for Mark McGuire's 70th home run ball started on eBay and finished in person in New York. There are more, including thousands of trading cards and other collectibles:
   —Big Ken Griffey, Jr. Collection $475.00
   —Mickey Mantle Signed Angelo Marino Lithograph $24.95
   —Autographed Preki Soccer Card $5.50

▶ Toys and Beanies. They still seem to be the rage whether they are action figures, games, fast food toys, or die cast metal soldiers:
   —Japanese Release Huge Godzilla! $36.00
   —Vintage Chewbacca Action Figure Carrying strap $24.99
   —Kicks the Soccer Bear $5.00

▶ Miscellaneous (such as garden items and tools). Everything else that wouldn't fit anywhere else!

—Complete Espresso Cafe Cost Over $55,000.00 only $5,000.00

—Magnetic Vehicle Signs—12 X 24 Under $40.00

—Rhus Aromatica, Fragra Seed $1.50

Remember that the prices you see next to these items are the most recent bid, not what the items have sold for.

Q10 What if I want to see just the subcategories under only one category?

Sure. Just click on the name of the category (which has no number in parentheses) and you will see all the subcategories listed. **Figure 1.5** shows the subcategories under Antiques.

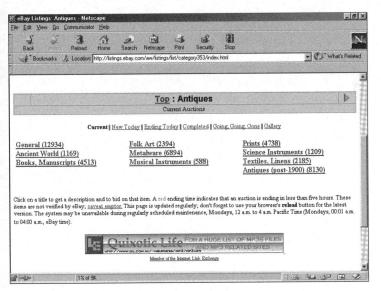

Figure 1.5 Each eBay category has subcategories as you can see here.

Now you can click on any one of these subcategories to get to the area you want. If you see more subcategories, just keep clicking until you get to the area you want. You can always go back; use the Back button on your Internet browser.

Abracadabra...where did that item go?

Items are always being added and deleted as auctions expire or as an item is sold or removed from an auction. Since the average visit to eBay is more than two hours, you expect things are hanging behind the scenes even as you are looking. To get the absolute latest when you are in any eBay screen, use the Reload or Refresh button on your browser. This reloads the page with the most current contents available. Just give it a click every now and then and you'll never be behind.

 It seems as though there are new categories every time I sign on. How can I keep up?

If it seems like there are new categories being added to eBay all the time, it's because there are! The eBay community is a dynamic one where offerings change constantly; this is what makes it exciting. Something is different every day in every category. The only way to keep up is to keep visiting new auctions as well as those you have visited before to check the status of items.

How is a new category added to eBay? If I have a great idea for one, what should I do with it?

The only way to add a new category or subcategory is to email eBay and make the suggestion. They will add that category if they think there is enough interest in a particular area. They might also add a new category if there is a grouping of similar items in another category and it would be easier for buyers and sellers to have those separate from one another. To write to them, go to the site map and click Contact eBay.

I've heard about a new eBay feature called the Gallery. It allows me to initially view pictures of items, rather than just a written description. What is it and how does it work?

Most items on eBay are offered within an auction using a written description and in some cases, there's a picture that accompanies the description. If you want more information about an item, you can just click on the description. The eBay folks are smart. They realize that if you can see what something looks like before you consider asking for more information, it might really make the right impression. They created the Gallery.

The Gallery is aptly named. Just like you would go to an art gallery to view certain works of art, the eBay Gallery offers you a special place to view other works—a showcase in which items are arranged in a visual catalog. The eBay people decide what goes into the Gallery, and an increasing number of items are turning up there.

In **Figure 1.6** you can see the Gallery entries for musical instruments. If you want more information, just click on the underlined description of a particular item; you are taken to the complete item description.

Figure 1.6 The Gallery offers visual as well as text information about an item.

The Gallery can be reached via the site map and sometimes there's a link on the home page that connects you to as well. Things may move slowly in the Gallery if your computer does not handle graphics quickly.

Getting Registered and Getting Started

Q14 I'm ready to take the plunge. How do I register?

You're almost ready to go. Just a bit about what it means to become registered as an eBay user.

Registration serves several purposes. First, it allows the people who run eBay to track their member's activities and make sure that these activities are kept within the scope of the user agreement (which you learn about later). Registration also provides you with your user ID, which is your screen name, and allows you to be identified online at all times. You'll see how important user IDs are when you want to determine how reliable a seller is and what kind of feedback others have offered about you.

Basic registration is really easy and consists of two simple steps: Completing the registration form and confirming your registration.

Registration Warning

Before you begin the registration process, be sure that you are using a computer where you also have access to your email. That way, you'll be able to check the confirmation of your registration immediately.

Follow these steps to start the registration process:

1. Go to the eBay Registration page. You can get there from the home page by clicking on REGISTER—It's Free and Fun.

2. As part of the registration process, the first thing you are asked is to select from a list which country you live in. Select the country and click the button labeled Begin the Registration Process Now.

3. Now it's time to complete the registration form you see in **Figure 1.7**. Throughout this form you will see some fields (such as Full Name) printed in green and have (required) next to them. These must be filled in for your registration to be complete. You need not fill in any information in a field that is not required. We'll only review the required fields.

Home Listings Buyers Sellers Search Help News/Chat Site Map

Try a new way to shop - browse Antique listings by photos.
What's new about Feedback Forum? Check it out!

eBay Registration

If you're not from the United States, click here.

How to Register - To register on eBay, follow the registration process below. When you complete all three steps, you can begin buying and selling on eBay.

1) Complete the eBay Initial Registration Form - Simply fill out the registration form below, review your information for accuracy, and click the Submit button.

2) Receive Confirmation Instructions - eBay will send you an e-mail message with a confirmation code.
If you already have completed step 1 and you need eBay to resend your confirmation instructions click here.

3) Confirm Your Registration - Once you have your access code (and your e-mail address), finalize your registration by accepting the eBay User Agreement and complete the eBay Confirm your Registration form.
If you have your confirmation code and you are ready to confirm your registration, click here.

Please Note: To be eligible to register, you must be over 18 years of age and provide valid contact information, including a valid e-mail address. **eBay** will not use any registration information for marketing, nor will we disclose this information to any outside party.

If you would like to read a full explanation of our privacy policy, click on the TRUSTe button below:

TRUSTe
site privacy statement

Step 1 - eBay Initial Registration Form

Simply fill out the information below and click the **continue** button.
Required entries are shown in green.

E-mail address e.g. username@aol.com	(required) *Note:* AOL and WebTV Users: Please remove any spaces from your username and add the domain suffix (@aol.com or @webtv.com to your username). For example, if your username is joecool, your e-mail address would be joecool@aol.com
Full name e.g., John H. Doe	(required) First M. Last
Company	(optional)
Address	(required)
City	(required)
State	Select State ▼ (required)
Zip Code	(required)
Primary phone # e.g., (408) 555 - 1234	( ) - (required) (extension)
Secondary phone #	( ) - (optional) (extension)
Fax #	( ) - (optional)

Figure 1.7 Here's where you begin the registration process.

—Enter your email address. Typing really counts here, so make sure that you get it correct. You must have an email address to participate in eBay.

—Use your mouse or press the Tab key to move down and complete the following fields:
   Address
   City
   State
   Zip Code
   Primary Phone

—Click the Continue button at the bottom of the form to register.

4. Once you click Continue at the bottom of the registration form, eBay shows you all the information you entered. You have a chance to review it and confirm that it is correct. If it is correct, click the Submit button (at the bottom of the form). You should see the Registration - Step 1 Complete! Notice as shown in **Figure 1.8**.

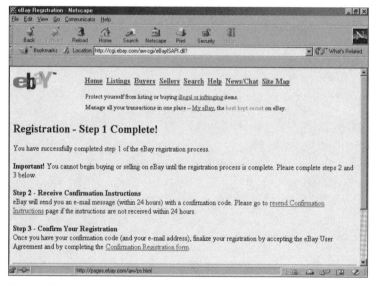

Figure 1.8 Step 1 is done—time to move on!

If the information that you provided is incorrect, click the Back button on your browser and make any corrections that you want; then click the button labeled Submit. That's all you need to do to complete the first step in the registration process. There's a whole bunch of other information that you could provide if you so choose. That's up to you.

eBay's Safety Net

eBay always gives you the chance to review what you have
entered when completing a form or a bid or are providing any
other information; it's their safety net. Type as carefully as you
can, but know that you always have a chance to use that
Back button to make changes.

5. Once the information that you entered is correct, you'll move
on to steps 2 and 3 of the registration process (**Figure 1.9**
shows step 3). You have to wait because your registration
application is now in eBay's hands. Check your email in the
next few minutes for your confirmation code and directions
from eBay regarding where to go to enter that code. If you
already had your confirmation number in hand, you could
click on the Confirmation Registration Form button you see
in Figure 1.8.

---

eb**Y**

Home Listings Buyers Sellers Search Help News/Chat Site Map

Try a new way to shop - browse Antique listings by photos.
What's new about Feedback Forum? Check it out!

Step 3 - Confirm Your Registration: Part 2 of 2

After you complete this form, your registration will be activated immediately, and you may begin
buying and selling on eBay.

Please note that you must create a **new** password now, which **must** be different from the
confirmation code sent to you in the confirmation instructions.

Your E-mail Address:	
The confirmation code sent to you in the confirmation instructions. Click here if you need eBay to resend your confirmation instructions.	
Create a **new**, permanent password:	
Type your **new** password again:	

Optional

| Choose a User ID (nickname): The User ID that you choose will become your "eBay name" that others see when you participate on eBay. You can create a name or simply use your email address. Examples "wunderkid", "jsmith98", "jeff@aol.com". | |

Complete your registration

Figure 1.9 You must confirm your eBay registration before it goes into effect.

No show, no go. I registered but I'm not there!

You must register to do anything on eBay other than browse. One mistake new eBay users make is completing the registration form, but never confirming their registration number (the last step); this leaves them unregistered. They sign on to eBay, try to buy or to set up an auction, and are told they don't exist! No reason to panic—you just have to go back to the registration area and finish the process.

Time for Lunch or a Pit Stop

You've finished part one of the registration process, but can't hang around and wait for the email confirmation. Remember, this confirmation contains the all-important code that you have to send to eBay to confirm that you are who you are. You're a busy person with lots to do and just can't keep the screen shown in Figure 1.9 on your monitor. To get back to the Web page shown in that figure, enter the following address in the Location line of your browser and you'll be ready to go:

http://cgi.eBay.com/aw-cgi/eBayISAPI.dll

You have your email message and it looks something like the one you see in **Figure 1.10**. The top of the message (Read *eBay Life...*) changes, so what you receive for an email, will not match perfectly what you see in Figure 1.10.

Dear leni@sunflower.com,

****

Read *eBay Life,* the new monthly community newsletter at

http://pages.eBay.com/aw/9902-pA1.html

****

Thank you for registering with eBay, the world's personal trading community! By receiving these confirmation instructions, you have completed step 2 of the registration process.

Please note that you cannot begin buying or selling on eBay until this confirmation process is complete.

To complete the registration process and to activate your account, follow these simple steps:

To complete the step 3 of the registration process, follow these simple instructions:

1. Print or write down this information as you will need it to confirm your registration:
   Your e-mail address is: leni@sunflower.com
   Your confirmation code: 5945
2. Go to the Confirm Your Registration page at
   http://pages.eBay.com/aw/US/reg-confirm.html
3. On that page, follow instructions to
   a) Agree to the eBay User Agreement, and
   b) Complete the Confirm Your Registration Form.

WebTV users—please visit the link below for instructions on accessing secure pages:

http://pages.eBay.com/aw/secure-webtv-support.html

Once you complete these steps, you can begin buying and selling on eBay!

Thank you for using eBay!
http://www.eBay.com

Figure 1.10 Here's your official letter—Welcome to eBay.

Click on the link that takes you to the Confirmation page
(**http://pages.eBay.com/aw/US/reg-confirm.html**), read the
long and boring and official user agreement, and click the
button labeled I Accept. If you decline, click the button labeled
I Decline.

The last step in the registration process requires you to
complete the information on the page you see in **Figure 1.11**.

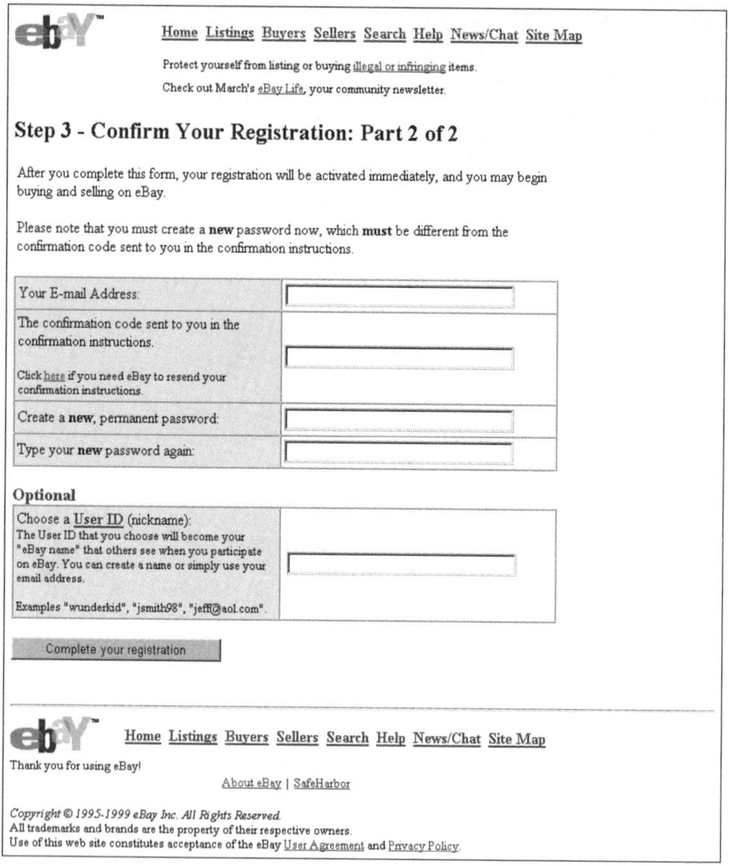

Figure 1.11 Here you will confirm your registration with eBay.

Here's what you need to enter:

▶ Your email address (again).

▶ The confirmation code that eBay sent you upon completion of the first step of the registration process. (In our example, as you can see in Figure 1.10, the code is 5945.)

▶ A new password. For a password, it is best to use random letters or numbers, but these (such as 4hf65tr) can be hard to remember. A good way to come up with passwords is to use a set of numbers, a symbol, and a word you remember. Like "linda#4931" where "linda" is your wife's name and "4931" are the last four digits of your social security number. If you use a word or short phrase, make sure that it is unrelated to your user ID or email address. Never make your password the same as your user ID or email address, as some ne'er-do-well might easily guess it and create all sorts of trouble for you.

▶ Your new password typed again (so eBay is sure it got it right).

▶ A user ID is optional. Your user ID has to be at least two characters long, cannot contain spaces, cannot be obscene, and you cannot use the @ symbol (saved for email stuff). Otherwise, you're free to use whatever you want.

If you don't choose to use a user ID, eBay will use your email address as your registration name. Why a user ID versus your email address?

A user ID gives you total flexibility regarding what you might want to use as an eBay name, as long as it doesn't violate eBay's rules (profanity, names such as Ronald Reagan, and the like). This means that if you're an eBayer who wants mostly to buy or sell books, you could have an ID like Bookhunter, Bookmaven, Usedbooks, or any combination of characters that indicate your interest. User IDs can be very cool. Just some of those currently in use include Lavajava, Poncho, Soapy, and Sublime.

On the other hand, you may want to just use your email
address, since it is easy to remember. You may not want to use
your email address because it's out there in the open for
everyone to see. User IDs are linked to email addresses, so
other eBay users can find your email address if they really want
to. But, non-eBayers cannot—so if you use your email address
as the user ID, it's likely that a browser could find your mail and
then add it to some inane list. It's just a matter of how public
you want your email address to be on the eBay screens.
However, you may also want to use a special email address
just for eBay. Most mail providers give you up to three
addresses, so you can dedicate one just to your eBay activity.

If you do elect to use a user ID, write it and the accompanying
password down and keep it in a safe place—just in case.

"Danger Will Robinson!" Lost Confirmation Code

You did everything exactly as you were supposed to, but you
lost the confirmation code that eBay sent you! No big deal.
You can go to **http://pages.eBay.com/aw/reqtemppass.html**
and enter your email address. eBay will gladly send you a
new one. What service!

Once you have completed this last part of the registration
process, click the Complete Your Registration button. You
should get the confirmation that you are a registered eBay
member. Congratulations!

What's with this legal agreement? Translation, please!

No matter how you look at it, eBay must have you agree to
some of the legal rules they think are important to running an
online auction.

It's not a perfect system, but such an agreement is necessary for you to participate. Basically, the agreement says that you are willing to pay for the service (only if you sell—not if you buy); that eBay is only a location where transactions can take place (and is not responsible for the quality or outcome of those transactions); that you are obligated as a buyer or seller to make good on your auction; and that you are being truthful in the information that you supplied during registration.

Any of these clauses, restrictions, and legalese are reasonable if you are a person who is interested in buying and selling, being honest, and having some fun (but never at the expense of other people).

Q16 What if I forget my user ID (I didn't write it down) or want to change it?

The first part of the question is easy to answer. Just use your email address instead of your user ID in transactions. Since eBay has a record of your email address (which has already been registered), it will know if you're the real you!

As to the second part of the question, you can change your user ID in a flash. Just go to the Change User ID page from the site map. Type in your old user ID, your password, and your new user ID (**Figure 1.12**). Your new user ID will be available instantly.

Please complete the following:

Your current User ID:

Your Password:

Your new User ID:

Figure 1.12 Changing your User ID is simple and instant.

**Q17** Changing a user ID seems almost too easy. Isn't that an invitation for dishonest eBayers to *hit and run*—create auctions, sell items, and then change IDs—never to be found?

You can only change your user ID once every 30 days. When you do change user IDs, a

follows the new ID around, telling all people who are interested that this member changed his or her ID in the last 30 days. While the shades icon is absolutely no reason to believe that the eBay member is nothing less than honest, it's a little flag that prompts you to ask if there is anything else (such as poor feedback, and the like) that you should keep a look out for? Also, user ID changes are not a frequent occurrence, so don't expect to see the shades icon often.

**Q18** The shades icon tells me that the eBay member changed user IDs. What else can I do with it?

If you click on it, you'll see the eBayer's entire ID history. Again, not many eBayers have any need to change their user ID, so you're not likely to see the shades icon often.

The eBay Community

Q19 I'm brand new to eBay and I'd like to find out more about eBay by "talking" with other eBay users. How can I do that?

The commitment to creating a genuine community has been taken very seriously by eBay and they make significant efforts to ensure that no member feels isolated. They figure that the friendlier eBay is, the more time people will spend on the site, and (of course) the more they might buy and sell.

The best place to start interacting with other eBay users is through one of the many eBay bulletin boards—and the one with the most inviting name—eBay Cafe.

eBay Cafe, shown in **Figure 1.13**, is a place for you to meet and interact with other eBay users. It's where you can leave messages and read other community member's responses. As you will see when you visit, it's also the place for jokes and anything else that members want to leave—but beware—there's no privacy here. What you enter into this interactive chat cafe is everyone's business since every eBay Cafe visitor has access to what it is you say.

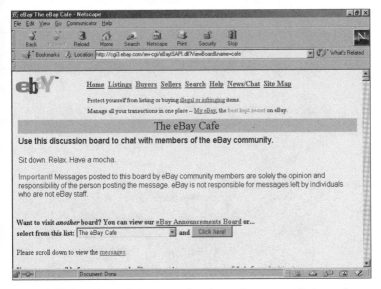

Figure 1.13 The eBay cafe is a great place just to browse and find out what other eBay users are discussing.

The eBay Cafe is also a great place to learn, since many of the very questions that you might have are probably occurring to other eBay members as well and being asked there.

To leave a message on the eBay Cafe, follow these steps:

1. Go to the eBay Cafe. You can do this by going to the site map link from any eBay page and then clicking eBay Cafe. For the cafe and other eBay locations that have URL's that are unlikely to change, it may be a good idea to bookmark these so they are easy to return to at a later time.

2. Scroll down on the page and enter your user ID.

3. Enter your password.

4. Enter the message you want to leave. eBay tells you that you are responsible for your own words, but it's worth repeating. After you enter your message, take a deep breath, wait a minute or two, and then reread what you have written. Be sure your message says what you want; the message is on its way to eBay and there's no recalling it when you click the button.

5. Click the button labeled **Save My Message!** The message will show up on the eBay Cafe for everyone who visits. The most recently entered message will appear at the top of the list and can show up within seconds of your saving it.

So many messages and so little time!

Lots of people like to leave messages at the eBay Cafe, but you may not want to read all of them. If you want to see fewer messages, use Reload and Show Me drop-down list, where you can specify whether you want to see all messages, those messages left within the last 24 hours, or those messages left within the last 6, 3, or 1 hours—or anywhere from the last 5 to the last 30 minutes.

What does a typical set of Cafe messages look like? Take a look at those in **Figure 1.14**. Here you see four messages, with identifying and other information across the top of each one. Take the message placed on the Cafe by max-n-mo and see what you can learn about this eBay member.

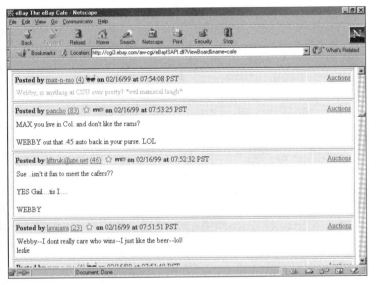

Figure 1.14 Some sample eBay cafe posting.

First, we can see that the message was posted by max-n-mo. If you want to email this eBayer, click on the underlined user ID. You'll are asked to provide your own user ID and password; you'll then see max-n-mo's email address and can click on it to send an email message.

Next, there's the number in parentheses indicating the amount of feedback that is available on this member. We talk about feedback starting with **Question 33**.

The shades icon is following the feedback count, meaning that the eBay member has changed email addresses in the last 30 days. Consider it a heads up.

Finally, there are the date and time of the post, followed by the message itself. If this eBay member is currently sponsoring an auction, you can click on the underlined Auction link (on the right edge of the message) and see what's up for sale, if anything.

On pancho's message you can see the Me icon standing for eBay's About Me feature (which you'll read about in **Question 56**) and a feedback star. The feedback star is a part of the comprehensive eBay feedback system.

Are there other bulletin boards that I can visit and leave messages on?

More than you can imagine. There's a bulletin board for the content in every category (such as coins and stamps), plus others of special interest such as the eBay Wanted Board (See **Question 31**).

Here's the list of current bulletin boards where you can leave messages within the eBay Cafe:

The eBay Q&A Board	The eBay Cafe
The eBay Support Q&A Board	Discuss eBay Newest Features
The eBay AOL Cafe	Live Support for New Users
Toys	Jewelry, Gemstones
Pottery, Porcelain	Computers
Trading Cards	Coins
Stamps	Dolls
Advertising Collectibles	Antiques
Beanies	Glass
Photo Equipment	Elvis
Emergency Contact	The New Board
Holiday	International Trading
Images/HTML	Comics
Sports	Garage
Die Cast	Music
Books	Movies
Furby	Canada's Board
United Kingdom Board	

I really like to be in the know. What's the latest going on at eBay and how do I find out?

Here's where the site map really comes in handy. If you want to know about what's really happening at eBay, there are several places you can turn to get different types of information.

To begin with, *eBay Life* is the first place you should go. This is easily reached from the site map, but is more easily reached via the home page. Just click on the *eBay Life* link (under the Fun Stuff icon); you'll see the daily newspaper from eBay as shown in **Figure 1.15** (which only shows the front page of this multipage electronic newspaper). There's tons of stuff that's always changing on the other *eBay Life* pages.

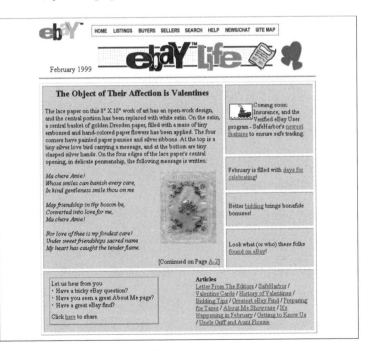

Figure 1.15 eBay Life is like your daily eBay newspaper—read it to keep up with changes on eBay including new features, new ideas and tips on using eBay.

For example, want to know about the absolutely newest eBay feature? This is where you'll find that information. How about letters to the editor? Bidding tips? Information about preparing taxes? *eBay Life* is definitely the place to go when you start becoming more familiar with the entire eBay site and what it offers. It's a great introduction to this growing and exciting community.

Want to be even more in the know? Check out the What's Happening at eBay? Web page, which you can get to by clicking Other Happenings on the home page. This summary of new things (shown in **Figure 1.16**) presents a hot link to each new area. If you have Daddy Warbucks on your side, why not go for one of the Big Ticket Items, such as the bed and breakfast that has an opening bid of $127,000; the new Plymouth Prowler for $44,000; or even a former Pepsi bottling plant that has a house to go along with it, for $5,000? What a deal!

Figure 1.16 Want to know what's happening? Go to What's happening, just as you see here.

What's Happening at eBay is also the place for special member deals, Club 99 (where items start for 99 cents), and For All Kids, the link to the For All Kids Foundation, for underserved and at-risk children.

 Are there other eBay features that can help me learn more about what's going on in the eBay community?

There sure are. A terrific place to get connected to the eBay community is through the News & Chat page, which you can also get to from the eBay home page by clicking the Get News & Chat icon. There are all kinds of information that you will find of value, some of the connections taking you to places already discussed, but several others as well. We'll focus on some of these in other places in *eBay Online Auctions*, but for now, here's a summary:

▶ News & Announcement tells you about eBay's more technical operations side and the latest features available. Customer Support is the Help wing of eBay. More about that later.

▶ It's "Welcome to the eBay Community!" where you really want to focus to learn more about eBay. This section of the site provides new and experienced users opportunities to learn much more about how eBay works directly from eBay support staff, as well as other eBay members. As you can see in **Figure 1.17**, there's something for everyone.

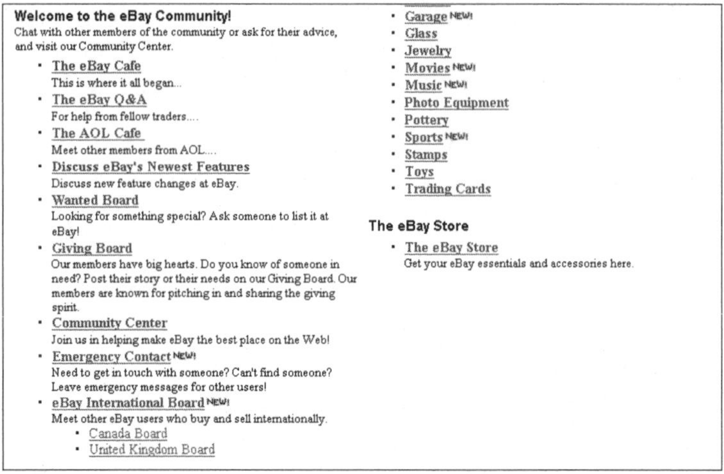

Figure 1.17 eBay tries to build a community from its members and starts with easily accessible features like the ones you see here.

Here's a description of what each one does:

▶ The eBay Cafe was described previously.

▶ The eBay Q&A is your opportunity to get assistance from other eBayers who are involved in buying and selling. You enter a message or an inquiry, and as with any bulletin board, everyone reading the eBay Q&A sees what you wrote. Here's a sample of the text from a few such messages that were posted. You should notice how diverse they are both in content and in tone, indicating that eBay is more or less a place where uncensored thinking and writing is supported:

> *"Michael and Billie—What excuses has the seller given you? Have you asked for a refund on the difference so you can be done with the deal? Maybe you can request their contact info and give them a phone call and discuss it."*

> *"Hope someone can give me some advice...Do you all think it would be appropriate to send an email to a 'new' bidder to reveal the reserve price on the item they bid on (at less than*

reserve?)...Opening bid is at $1.00, but reserve is only $5.00...I'm thinking they may not understand the reserve price thing. Would that be too intrusive?"

"Wonder if anyone has good advice on the Sony Mavica 71 model camera...Thinking about purchasing that model for items too large to scan. If you have had experience with it, would you give me a thumbs up? or down? Thanks. Fred"

▶ The AOL Cafe is a way for eBay members to meet other eBay members who also belong to America Online (AOL), popular commercial Internet provider.

▶ Discuss eBay's Newest Features allows you communicate with eBay staff regarding recent and proposed eBay features. There's a drop-down menu of different eBay features and items and you can select the one of your choice, send an email message to eBay personnel and expect an answer within a reasonable amount of time. Sometimes minutes, sometimes more, but never usually more than 24 hours.

▶ Want something but can't find it on eBay? Go to the Wanted Board. Here you'll be able to see what other eBayers want and perhaps you can accommodate them.

▶ The Welcome to the eBay Community section contains the Giving Board, where you can help less fortunate people by seeing if eBay members can help through deeds and contributions.

Any one of these sections will give you information about what's happening at eBay; reviewing them all will keep you very well informed. Check at least once a week so you are not caught off guard and remain well informed. Remember, a well-informed eBay member is one who enjoys and benefits from his or her membership.

I'm really confused and can't seem to find an answer anywhere I look. What kind of help can I get?

There's not an eBayer who does not need help at one point or another. Where's the best place to start? The Help Desk, of course. You can get there by clicking Help (at the top of the eBay home page).

▶ Starting Point is perfect for beginners since it gives you a place to start when you don't even know what your first question might be.

▶ New to eBay? is for first timers and here you can learn a little about what eBay is as well as how it works; you can get detailed instructions on all the main topics, including browsing, searching, bidding, setting up an account, and more. You'll find helpful tutorials here.

▶ Topics is like the site map; here, however, you get help on a topic rather than going to the topic itself. As you can see in **Figure 1.18**, information about every aspect of eBay is organized into categories and is easily accessible through one click of the mouse.

▶ Where do you find answers to the most frequently asked questions about eBay? FAQ. For example, if you want to know about different types of auctions, go to the FAQ and click Auction Format; you get two pages explaining the differences between reserve, private, Dutch, and the other types of auctions used on eBay.

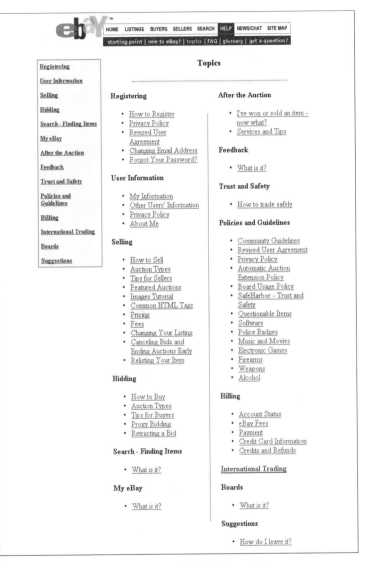

Figure 1.18 Need Help? You're sure to find the right topic here.

▶ The Glossary in this book provides definitions for eBay terms.

▶ In a quandary? Got a Question? offers 24-hour support from real people! Got a Question? is organized into the following general categories to help you focus on where you can best get help fastest:

—Trust and Safety.

—General Support Q&A Board.

—Live Support for New Users.

—User-to-User eBay Q&A Board, where you can get support from other eBay users.

—Images/HTML Board for help using images in your auctions.

—A Search box at the top of the Got a Question? Page so you can go off on your own and search out topics. Just enter key words (such as "bid") or a question (such as "How do I bid?") and click on the Search button. This is a very general search engine, so you're sure to get lots of possibilities.

eBay—Just for Me

Q24 eBay seems to be a nice place to see what other people are up to in their collecting and such. Is there a way I can introduce myself to others or find out about other eBay users?

So many people are using eBay on a regular basis (more than 500,000), there had to be a way to make it as friendly as possible. One way is through the relatively new feature About Me.

This icon shows up in various places throughout your eBay travels. It means that the eBay member has gone to the trouble to design and make public a personal profile such as the one you see in **Figure 1.19**.

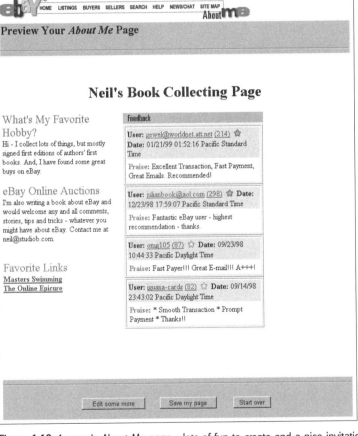

Figure 1.19 A sample About Me page—lots of fun to create and a nice invitation to other eBayers to learn something of a more personal nature.

Your About Me page (it actually becomes a Web page with an Internet address) can take on one of several appearances and contain all different types of information. In fact, once it is created you can edit particular aspects using HTML, the language used to create Web pages. Creating your own About Me page is easy and fun and it's surprising that more eBayers don't do it.

There are only a few steps to completing an About Me page. First, you need to select a layout you like. Second, add the information you want. Finally, save your About Me page. You can go back and edit it at any time. Follow these steps to create your own About Me page:

1. Click on the site map by the eBay logo on any eBay Web page. Click About Me, which is located under Registered User Services.

2. Enter your user ID. Remember that you can use your email address if you don't have a user ID.

3. Enter your password and click the button labeled Create and Edit Your Page.

4. Click on the button that corresponds to the type of layout you want to use for your About Me page. In this example, we clicked the two-column layout option.

   There are three types of layout: two-column, newspaper, and centered. The example you see in Figure 1.19 is a two-column layout. Which one for you? Perhaps the best answer is which you think looks the best; they can all contain the same amount of information.

5. Enter the information that will be displayed on your About Me page.

   The form that you use to do this is shown in **Figure 1.20**.

Advanced Pages Welcome

Advanced eBay users can opt to create their own layout and format for their About Me page using HTML. For example, a page can be created using Microsoft FrontPage (or any HTML editor) and then copied the <body> ... </body> section and pasted it into eBay's page editor.

HOME   LISTINGS   BUYERS   SELLERS   SEARCH   HELP   NEWS/CHAT   SITE MAP   About me

About Me As easy as 1, 2, 3
Step 2 Pick elements to include in your About Me page.

Select different elements you'd like to include on your About Me page. You can choose any combination of elements. These will be arranged according to the layout you chose from **Step 1**.

Personalize Your Page

Page Title Create a title for your page.	Title:	
Welcome Message Create a short paragraph to welcome visitors to your page.	Heading:	
	Text:	
Another Paragraph What else do you want to share with others?	Heading:	
	Text:	
Picture Link to a picture that you've posted on the Web.	Caption:	
	URL:	http://

Show Your eBay Activity

Feedback Display your feedback comments.	Show 10 most recent comments ▼
Items for Sale Display your current items for sale which will appear oldest to most recent.	Caption: Show no items ▼

Share Some of Your Favorite Things

Favorite Links Help others find your favorite places on the Web.	Name:	
	URL:	http://
	Name:	
	URL:	http://
	Name:	
	URL:	http://
Favorite eBay Items Share your eBay "finds" with others.	Item #:	Check it out! ▼
	Item #:	Check it out! ▼
	Item #:	Check it out! ▼

Preview your page	Choose new layout
(Go to step 3)	(Go back to step 1)

Figure 1.20 The About Me form.

Here's a summary of the information that's needed and what it does. You can see examples of each in Figure 1.19. You'll be able to go back and make corrections, but try to get your spelling right the first time.

About Me Element	What It Does
Page Title	Places a title at the top of the page. This is the first thing that other eBayers see when then look at your About Me Page.
Welcome Message	This message provides information about your page to all visitors.
Another Paragraph	Add anything you want here that will tell visitors about you or about what you like to collect or sell.
Picture	Any picture here can work, such as your favorite portrait, one of that Model T you're restoring or of Pepper, the Labrador that sits by your side when you buy and sell trading cards.
Feedback	If you want visitors to see recent feedback about you, use this drop-down menu to identify how much feedback. Select the Show No Feedback option if that's what you want.
Items for Sale	Want to let visitors know what you have for sale? Enter a caption and indicate how many you want to feature.
Favorite Links	Enter up to three of your favorite Internet links, perhaps to another Web page that has information about your collection, a hobby, or even your family tree.
Favorite Items	Enter the item number of the eBay items that you've seen on sale that you really like. This is a great place to show off your good taste!

6. Click the button labeled Preview Your Page (at the bottom of the About Me page). You'll see exactly what your page would look like had it been accessed by a visitor.

7. Now you can do one of four things:

   —Click Edit to continue the editing process. This takes you back to the screen from which you just came.

   —Click Save My Page to complete the About Me creation process; save your page to eBay and get your own URL.

   —Click Edit Using HTML to use the HTML (Hypertext Markup Language) to make additional fancy changes in your About Me page).

   —Start over if you've created a monster and want to start again.

8. You're done editing; click Save My Page. eBay wants you to confirm that you are done editing and really want to save the page; or would you rather continue editing? Click the appropriate button.

Forgot That URL?

In your About Me page setup, you need to enter different URLs (if you want to) so that eBay knows what to display on the About Me page. What should you do if you are in the middle of creating the About Me page and have to find the URL? Search for the URL either using a search engine or go to the page for which you need the URL using a bookmark that you established earlier. Cut or copy the URL using the right mouse button, use the Back key on your browser to return to the setup page for About Me, and paste the URL. Another way is to just start another browser session and use it to find the locations you want, then copy the URL from the location window and paste it into the other (eBay) browser session.

Easy, no?

In **Figure 1.21** you can see eBay's notification that your About Me page is ready to share with others. It even has its own URL so you can access it when outside the eBay system!

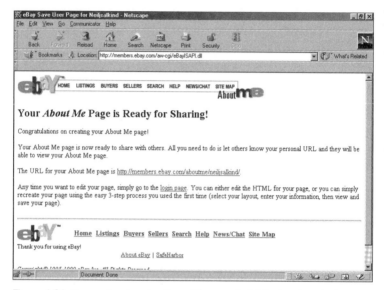

Figure 1.21 Your notice that the About Me page is finished and ready for everyone to see.

Want to go to your eBay About Me page at any time? Go to the site map, click About Me, and enter your user ID and password. Best of all, your eBay transactions are now accompanied by this cool graphic telling everyone at eBay that they can find out more about you with a click.

You're ready to move on to the next section of *eBay Online Auctions* and learn all about buying and making a bid and checking on the status of your efforts. In fact, being a good buyer is important in and of itself, but it's also the best way to learn how to be a good seller. That way, you'll know what a buyer's expectations are and how to design your auctions so they have appeal.

Section 2

Buying

Buying

Buying

Buying

Buying

ying

2

Buying

By this time you should be signed up and fully registered as a member of the eBay community. You should also have some idea of how eBay is organized and where you can find information about what you might need help on.

This chapter contains information about what is probably the most exciting and certainly the most central of all eBay activities: Buying. Imagine sitting in front of your computer and waiting for the allotted time for an auction to run out, knowing that if your most recent and highest bid is not bettered, then that replica Louis XIV side table is yours for only $367.00! You frantically push the Reload button on your Web browser. Again and again. The time is running out; 1:45 remaining in the auction. (Push.) 1:13 remaining. (Push.) 22 seconds! (Push.) The auction is over and the table is yours!

We start this section with a discussion of browsing and searching on eBay to find what you want. We tell you what to do if what you want is not available: You could encourage some seller to offer the item! Then we move on to making bids—placing an offer for an item—and all the things you can do to maximize your chances of getting the items that you want. We also teach you about eBay's feedback system and how you can be sure that the eBayer who is selling or buying has a reputation for being reliable. We end this section with a discussion of eBay's rapid movement into the global market and how you can bid (and maybe even win) confidently, even across international borders.

Browsing and Searching

 **I'm new to eBay and not looking for anything in particular. All I want to do is browse around and see what's out there. Any advice?**

You're one of millions of people who are not quite ready to buy or sell until you've gotten the lay of the land. In other words, you want to be very familiar with what's out there before you even begin thinking about buying. Let's do a little browsing.

Good browsers, or **lurkers** as they are sometimes good-naturedly referred to, feel comfortable just looking around eBay and taking in the sights. In this case, that includes the many categories and subcategories that are available and that were described in "Getting Started" of this book.

You can find the main eBay categories in several locations. Once you get to any list, you can click on the category to reveal it's contents and scroll through to see the various items. Locations where categories can be explored are as follows:

▶ The eBay home page where the main categories are listed along the left side of the opening screen. A click on any one of these takes you to subcategories. A click on any subcategory takes you to the list of items that are currently being offered at auction. For example, in **Figure 2.1,** you can see a list of items available in the Collectibles subcategory Bottles.

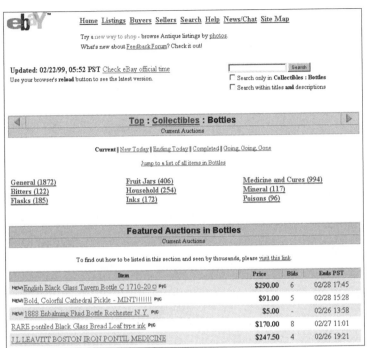

Figure 2.1 Each one of these subcategories represents an auction and within an auction you can have one or a thousand items.

▶ On the Listings page (click Listings on the eBay home page), you can find subcategories along with featured and hot items. **Featured items** are those that appear at the top of an auction; the seller pays an extra fee for that prominent placement. **Hot items** are those for which more than 30 bids have been placed. They're the items in most demand on a particular day. We'll talk about that more in a moment.

▶ Click eBay Categories or eBay Categories Overview. You'll find it on the site map link at the top of any eBay page (under Current Listings).

Since the Listings link provides the most comprehensive
collection of categories, take a look at what's contained on
such a page (**Figure** 2.2).

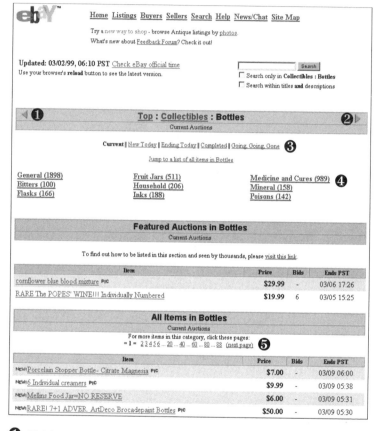

❶ Click here to go to the previous subcategory

❷ Click here to go to the next subcategory

❸ Click here to navigate though an auction

❹ Subcategories

❺ Click here to go to other pages

Figure 2.2 Items are listed under a variety of different headings such as Featured
Auctions and All Items...

The category name (Collectibles: Bottles) appears at the top of the page with triangles at each end of the title bar. Click on the right one to go to the next category in the listings and click on the left triangle to go to the previous category in the listing. If the user goes into one of the subcategories beneath the secondary categories (like General, for example), the left triangle (the "previous" arrow) disappears. Don't panic! There's just no place to go back to when you are at the beginning.

All the Bottles subcategories are shown below the title bar. They are all linked to that area on eBay that contains the descriptions of these items. You can tell how many items are in each subcategory by looking at the number to the right of each subcategory. For example, Figure 2.2 shows that there are 511 items in the Fruit Jars subcategory.

The seller pays an extra fee for a featured auction, which contains items that get extra attention. These items appear at the top of each opening auction page.

You can also see the complete listing of all items in this particular category and subcategory. The example you see in Figure 2.2 indicates that there are 83 pages of bottles. At 50 items per page, we're talking more than 4,000 bottles of every shape, size, and color. These 4,000 bottles represent hundreds of different sellers.

You can find the hot items at the bottom of the page (which are not shown in Figure 2.2). You can make use of several different eBay tools while navigating through these 88 pages.

You can click on any one of the following links:

▶ The Current link shows you the items in the auction.

▶ New Today link shows you the items that have been added today.

▶ Ending Today link shows you all the items in auctions that will end today.

▶ The Completed link shows you the items in auctions that have ended in the last 30 days. This is a great way to check and see what those items you didn't bid on finally sold for. It gives you a good idea of the current value of items being sold on eBay.

▶ The Going, Going, Gone link shows you auctions that are ending in the next five hours. The ending time appears in red.

▶ Immediately below the links at the top of the page is a link (Jump to a list of all items in Bottles) that takes you directly to the list of items in this auction.

Since all the items don't fit on any one page, eBay has a neat page tool for skipping pages. This set of page numbers appears immediately after the All Items In heading as well as at the bottom of the page as you see in **Figure** 2.3.

Figure 2.3 Click on these triangles to skip pages of items and move forward or backward in the listing of total items.

The bottom of the page also shows the same information so that you can click and quickly get to a specific page of items, but it also contains another set of triangular shape buttons that take you to the next or previous page. If you want to browse through page after page of items, this is one easy way to do it.

 When I get to the items to browse, I see sections titled Featured Auctions and Hot Items. What are they?

Both Featured Auctions and Hot Items are special categories. **Featured Auctions** are those that the seller pays eBay an extra $99.95 when the item is listed and placed in this special location. The logic is that if the listing for the item is right up front, potential buyers will more quickly see it and bid on it. Items that are set apart from others might catch the eBayer's eye. There's nothing special about items listed in this section other than that the seller wants them placed there. These items do, however, typically cost more than $99.95.

Hot Items are those items that have received more than 30 bids. It's eBay's way of telling you that these items have a special significance, which could be price, condition, or rarity. eBay thinks that these items are particularly interesting for people visiting this auction and places them in their own category. It's also an award for offering an appealing item at an appealing minimum bid.

Section 2 Buying

Now I know how to navigate and understand the eBay auction system. What's all the information I see next to items?

Welcome to Item Anatomy 101. In **Figure 2.4** you can see the listing for several different mineral bottles items in the Bottles auction. Look at each item element as it is listed.

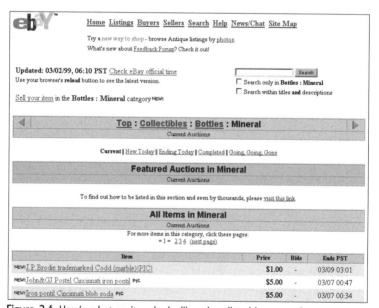

Figure 2.4 Here's what an item looks like when listed in an auction.

▶ *Item.* Contains a title for the item. The seller creates this and a good title tells you enough to pique your interest.

▶ *Price.* This shows the most recent price bid for that item. This is not necessarily the price that the seller is hoping for, but rather, what some other bidder is willing to pay.

▶ *Bids.* This represents the number of bids received for the item.

▶ *Ends PST.* This indicates when the auction ends—in Pacific Standard Time. Remember that if you are not on the West coast of the United States (or darn close to it), the time the clock shows on your computer (or on your wall) is hours different. The auction will end in PST, so adjust your timing and bidding accordingly. You can always click on the Check eBay Official Time link at the top of the page to synchronize your watch.

The graphics shown in Figure 2.4 were all placed by eBay on behalf of sellers to attract attention to the item. Some cost money, others don't. The

indicates that this item is new to this auction and stays on the item description for 24-hours. The "pic" graphic indicates that there is a picture accompanying the complete item description (See **Question 44**)

Following an Auction? Reload Often!

One important element in an item description line is to remember the time in which an auction ends (at the end of the line shown in Figure 2.4). Since this is a true indicator of how much time is left to bid, the amount of time left in an auction is always changing. It won't change on your screen unless you use your browser's Reload or Refresh button. Clicking that button updates everything, including the number of bids on an item as well as the time left. When things get down to the wire (less than an hour to go, when the time appears in red), you'll want to know exactly how much time is left before you make that final bid. Reload or refresh (as the case might be) often.

**I just want to fool around and see what's on eBay. Do I have to bid?**

Absolutely not. You're welcome to browse or lurk to your heart's content. When it comes time to make a bid, you will be required to enter your user ID and password and a price at which you want to bid. You are then allowed to preview your bid before it is finalized.

What if I can't find exactly what I want? Is there a way to search for it?

A great question with a long answer. Clearly, you will more often be looking for a particular item (such as that 1953 Rolls Royce Silver Shadow) rather than browsing around through hundreds or thousands of categories.

There are several ways to search for an item using eBay's search tools. Let's go through each of those tools, how they work and what how they are best used.

The Simple Search

This is the easiest and quickest way to search the entire eBay site. The fact that it is simple to use does not mean that it isn't powerful. The simple search takes place on the eBay home page in the Search box.

The steps are a cinch:

1. Type in any words you want eBay to search for. The more specific you are, the more narrow the search will be. If the specified item is available on eBay, you'll find it. You can use one or several words.

2. Click search.

A search for a Bose Wave radio results in what you see in
Figure 2.5. You see the item number, a brief description, the
price, the number of bids made on the item, and what time the
auction ends for each item. Looks like there are some good
prices; think I might bid.

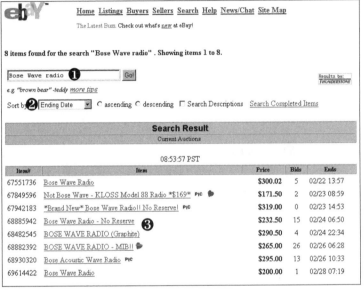

❶ What you searched for

❷ How the results of the search are sorted

❸ The results of the search

Figure 2.5 The results of a simple search shown.

This was a successful search because we knew exactly what we were looking for. If we used this simple method and searched only using the word *radio*, we would have found 4,922 items! Rule number one is to provide as much information as possible.

Search On!

Want to start another search? No reason to return to the home page. Many eBay pages have a Search box at the top, such as the one shown in the top-left corner of Figure 2.4. Just enter the words you want to search for and click the button labeled Go!

Making Your Searches More Precise

You can enter words in the Search box on eBay's home page and get close to what you want—if you can accurately describe it. You can be even more precise in this little Search box and perform some very powerful searches. **Table 2.1** gives you some examples of what you can enter in the Search box you see in Figure 2.5 and what you would find if you're looking for a wave radio. Remember: If you do not check Search Within Titles and Descriptions before you push the Search button, eBay only searches the title of each item, not the lengthy descriptions of each item.

Table 2.1—Example Search: A Wave Radio

You Type	This Is What You Find
wave radio	Any item that includes the words *wave* and *radio,* regardless of order.
(wave, radio)	Any item that contains the word *wave* or *radio.*
"wave radio"	The exact phrase *wave radio.*
wave-radio	Occurrences of the word *wave,* but not accompanied by radio.
wave *	Items that include the word wave and anything following the word wave, such as *wave radio, book of wave functions,* and *Phantom Menace New Figures Wave Pre-sell.* The * is a wild card that allows a search for anything. Entering the characters 198* would search for items with 1980, 1981, 1982, and so on in the description.
* wave	Items that include the word *wave* and anything preceding the word *wave,* such as *Coca-Cola playing cards (wave)* or *The Third Wave Toffler.*
wave-(radio, functions)	The word wave, but not the words *radio* or *functions.*

Section 2 Buying

Always try to narrow your search terms, not only in words, but the ideas as well. For example, say you're looking for rare coins—in particular a steel penny from the 1940s. A search on the word *penny* reveals 1,128 items, but a search (on titles only) on 194* steel penny (the * gets you all of the 1940s) reveals five exact matches:

▶ 1943 Lincoln Steel Penny Set

▶ 1943 U.S. Steel Penny Mint Set

▶ Punched Steel Penny Strip, from 1943, 3X5 NR

▶ 1943 Steel Cents (PENNY)

▶ 1943 Steel Penny PCI 66

Seek and Ye Shall Find, or Find Something Better!

A true story: Sam was searching for a book by the illustrator Arthur Szyk. Instead of typing in *szyk* which is the correct spelling, he entered *syzk*, a simple switching of letters. Rather than finding nothing (which should have happened since the spelling was incorrect), one seller had inadvertently misspelled the name the same way when she created her auction—it came up as the result of the search! Lo and behold, there was only one bid since no other prospective buyers found the item when they searched using the correct spelling. The rule? Check your spelling carefully when you are searching and when you are titling. This mistake was a fortunate one for the bidder (he got the opening low price), but not for the seller. The same item sold for five times as much in another auction.

The Mega-Power Search Engine!

If you want to go from the simple to the very extensive as far as search options go, this is the place. eBay's search engine, shown in **Figure 2.6**, allows you to search for items in so many different ways, that it would probably be impossible to miss something that's really there.

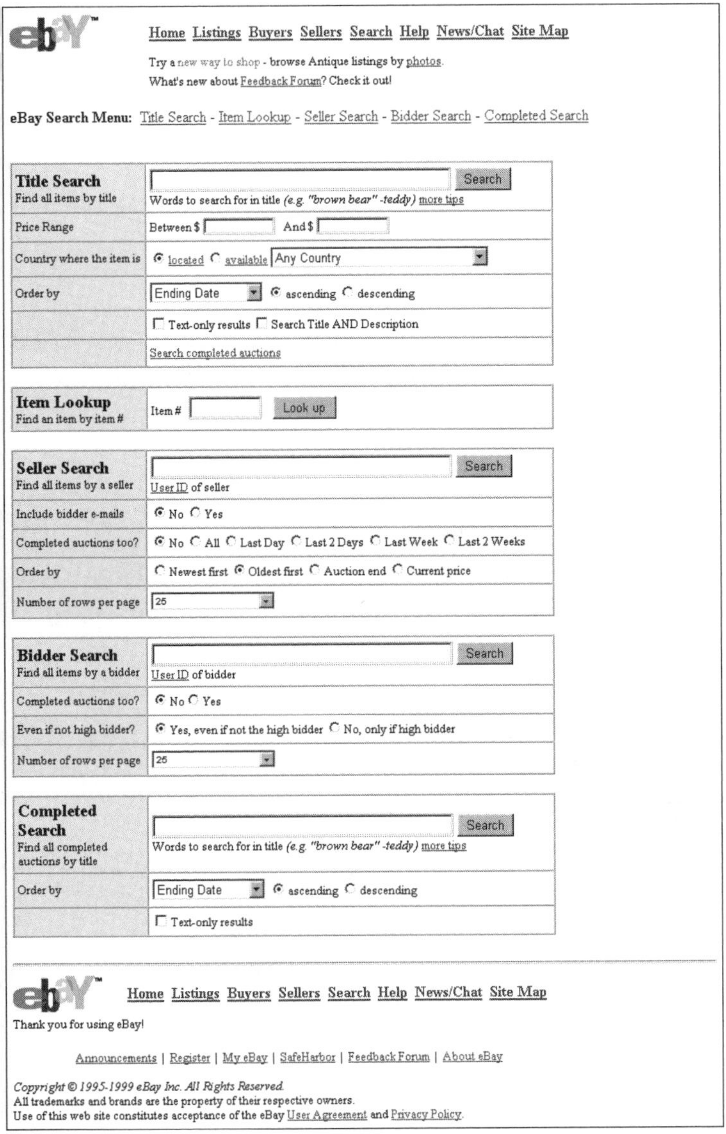
Home Listings Buyers Sellers Search Help News/Chat Site Map

Try a new way to shop - browse Antique listings by photos.
What's new about Feedback Forum? Check it out!

eBay Search Menu: Title Search - Item Lookup - Seller Search - Bidder Search - Completed Search

Title Search Find all items by title	[ ] Search Words to search for in title *(e.g. "brown bear" -teddy)* more tips
Price Range	Between $ [ ] And $ [ ]
Country where the item is	located available Any Country
Order by	Ending Date ascending descending
	Text-only results Search Title AND Description
	Search completed auctions

Item Lookup Find an item by item #	Item # [ ] Look up

Seller Search Find all items by a seller	[ ] Search User ID of seller
Include bidder e-mails	No Yes
Completed auctions too?	No All Last Day Last 2 Days Last Week Last 2 Weeks
Order by	Newest first Oldest first Auction end Current price
Number of rows per page	25

Bidder Search Find all items by a bidder	[ ] Search User ID of bidder
Completed auctions too?	No Yes
Even if not high bidder?	Yes, even if not the high bidder No, only if high bidder
Number of rows per page	25

Completed Search Find all completed auctions by title	[ ] Search Words to search for in title *(e.g. "brown bear" -teddy)* more tips
Order by	Ending Date ascending descending
	Text-only results

Home Listings Buyers Sellers Search Help News/Chat Site Map

Thank you for using eBay!

Announcements | Register | My eBay | SafeHarbor | Feedback Forum | About eBay

Copyright © 1995-1999 eBay Inc. All Rights Reserved.
All trademarks and brands are the property of their respective owners.
Use of this web site constitutes acceptance of the eBay User Agreement and Privacy Policy.

Figure 2.6 The mother of all eBay search tools!

How do you get there? Click on the Search link at the top of any eBay page. Note, however, that the five different search areas are all for heavy-duty searching. If all you want to do is search for the name of a particular item, you should not have to go beyond the Search box.

Here is a description of what options and search tools are available:

▶ In the Title Search area, you can search by:

—The title of an item that allows you to search descriptions as well as titles. It doesn't have to be exact, but once again, the more exact the information, the easier it will be for eBay to find an item.

—A price range.

—The country where the item is located.

—Whether the resulting list of items is ordered by last date first (**ascending**) or most recent date first (**descending**).

▶ You can enter a number in the Item Lookup area (one that you might have written down while browsing) and then click Look Up.

▶ In the Seller Search area you can search via the following methods:

—All the items that are being offered by a particular seller. This allows you to return quickly to your favorite sellers who regularly have the stuff you want.

—You can also include emails from others who have bid on a particular item, completed auctions and their closing dates and how many rows you want to show on each page.

▶ In the Bidder Search area you can search with these
methods:

—The User ID of a bidder (check up on what your
archenemy eBayer who outbid you last time is up to)

—You can also specify whether you want to search on only
those auctions that were completed, whether the person
was the high bidder, and how many rows you want to
show on each page.

—Finally, you can find all of the auctions already complete
(under Completed Search), as well as order these auctions
by completion date.

To Power Search or Not? That Is the Question.

Is it necessary to use the powerful and flexible search engine
that eBay provides? Not necessarily. If you know what you're
looking for and have some idea how it will appear in an
item description, the simple Search box at the top of many
eBay pages should be all you need. If you want to make
sure that your Uncle Moe (user ID: unclemoeiscool) is not
selling the old comic collection that you left at his house,
you could do a seller search. Most often, however, good
narrow searching using the techniques and ideas discussed
earlier should suffice.

 I'd like to see my search results displayed in something other than the order of the auction end date. Can I do this?

Yes, and quite easily. After you complete an initial search, you can ask eBay to order the search according to several different criteria (**Figure 2.7**). This search box is located at the top of results of any previous search.

Figure 2.7 Sorting the results of a search in one of many different ways.

For example, say that your search revealed Beanie Baby auctions and your Beanie Baby budget is no more than $40.00. If you sorted on the bid price in ascending order, you'd see the Babies with the lowest bid price listed first. That way, you can see what's available within a certain bid range without having to scroll and page through the entire list.

On the other hand, if you sorted the list in descending order (from highest to lowest), you'd find the Princess Diana Beanie starting for a tidy $90,000. You can also sort by the end date of the auction (which is the default) and the **search ranking**. This is a rank based on the number of search terms found in the search—the same way some Internet search engines rank by how close the found site matches your search request.

 What if I want to buy something that's not listed in any category? Is there some way to let others know what I'm looking for?

That's what the Wanted Page is for. To find it, click on the site map link at the top of any eBay page and then click on the

Wanted Page link listed under Buyer Services, Bidding Management. The Wanted Page looks a lot like the eBay Cafe. You leave a message describing what you are looking for; other eBayers might let you know where that particular item is located. Here are some excerpts from the eBay Wanted Board:

▶ "Looking for front page of the *San Francisco Chronicle* or *Examiner* dated April 7, 1954. Will bid or buy."

▶ "Looking for snowshoes. Prefer Atlas 1033 model or similar model for Tubbs or Redfeathers."

▶ "I don't know if this exists but I am looking for a price guide for items from Danbury Mint and Franklin Mint. Or, if you know of a place online to go for information [please notify me]. I have hit a dead end. Thanks."

▶ "Wanted: ANYTHING for my MARGARET MITCHELL collection: articles, clippings, photos, postcards, etc. Also any old articles about or reviews of GWTW (book, not movie). Permanent want. Thanks!"

▶ "Found some very old toys...metal ones it looks like ... cowboys and Indians and some G.I.'s...and some cars and airplanes...found an airplane made by Tootsie Toys? Can anyone help me out with my dilemma? Thanks for your time and your help."

Of course, these statements are accompanied by the eBay user's ID so they can be easily contacted.

Posting such notes may lead to a contact from someone who wants to offer you a direct buy rather than going through eBay and paying the commission. It's best to just respond to them and tell them that circumventing eBay is against eBay's rules and that you would rather participate in a legitimate auction.

Section 2 Buying

Feedback: Knowing Who You're Dealing With

 **I'm ready to plunk down my hard-earned cash. How do I make sure that the seller is reliable?**

Perhaps eBay's best feature is Feedback, which is where both buyers and sellers can leave feedback about their transactions. The most important eBay rule for both beginners and experienced auction participants? If you have not dealt with a particular buyer or seller before, you owe it to yourself to review the feedback about their previous eBay transactions.

There are three main things buyers will want to tell other eBayers:

▶ Did the seller communicate well through email?

▶ Was the item sent on time?

▶ Did the item arrive in the expected condition?

There are three main things sellers will want to tell other eBayers:

▶ Did the buyer respond to email quickly?

▶ Was the debt paid quickly?

▶ Were there any problems with the transaction (such as a bad check)?

Feedback is such an important part of using eBay, that there exists an entire forum just to handle that topic. You can find the Feedback Forum on the site map (under Registered User Services). Click the Feedback Forum link and you'll see something similar to what's shown in **Figure 2.8**.

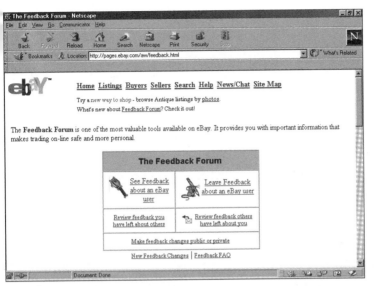

Figure 2.8 Leave your comments at The Feedback Forum. It's a critical place to visit when selling or buying.

The Feedback Forum allows you to

▶ See feedback about another eBay user (seller or buyer)

▶ Leave feedback about another eBay user (seller or buyer)

▶ See the feedback that you left

▶ See the feedback that other eBay users left you

We'll talk about each one of these in a moment, but first let's get to the most important task: getting feedback about a seller.

Q33 How can I discover feedback about any eBay user?

eBay allows you to find feedback for any eBay user through the Feedback Forum in Figure 2.8. Follow these steps:

1. Click on the See Feedback About an eBay User link on the Feedback Forum screen. You'll see the screen shown in **Figure 2.9**.

2. Enter the user ID for whom you want feedback.

3. Click on the amount of feedback you want to see.

4. Click Button. You'll see the feedback profile about that person such as that shown in **Figure 2.10**.

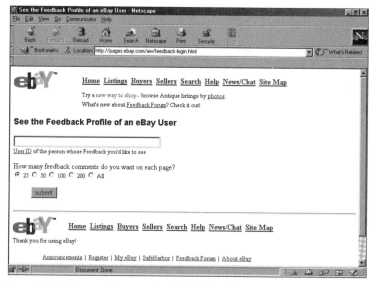

Figure 2.9 Getting ready to see the feedback profile of any eBay user.

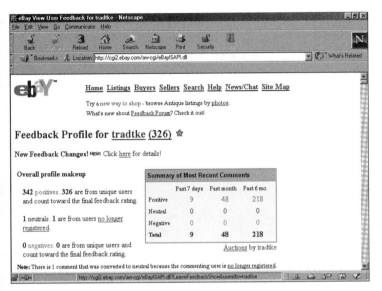

Figure 2.10 A sample feedback profile.

In the example shown here, user ID tradtke received a total of 342 feedbacks, 326 of which were from **unique people**. That means that 326 people contributed feedback (and there were 16 repeat leavers of feedback). All 342 were positive, with 9 occurring in the past 7 days, 48 in the past month, and 218 within the past 6 months.

Remember that the feedback number alone can be a bit misleading. An eBayer gets one point added to the total rating for a positive feedback and one point taken away for negative feedback. For example, a feedback number of 15 might indicate that someone got positive feedback from 15 eBayers; it could also mean that the same user got positive feedback from 30 eBayers and negative feedback from 15 (for a total of 30–15). The number alone is not necessarily a good indicator. Rather, you need to look at the distribution of positives, neutrals, and negatives over time (as shown in Figure 2.10).

Even if the feedback is positive, you might want to know exactly what was said. Keep reading down the Feedback page (**Figure 2.11**) to see what others have said about this eBay user. You can see positive feedback such as "Quick payment" and "GREATEST BUYER EVER." Not bad.

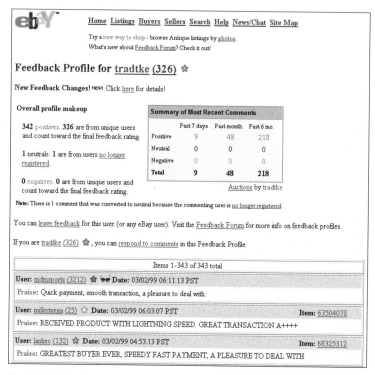

Figure 2.11 Seeing the contents of the feedback profile for an eBay user.

Q34 Any other way to see an eBayer's feedback profile?

You can go to an eBayer's feedback profile by clicking anywhere in eBay on the number that accompanies that user's ID. tradtke (326) is shown in **Figure 2.12**. You'll also notice that the high bidder's profile can be checked by clicking on the 22 to the right of the user ID.

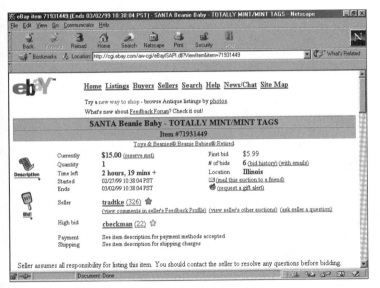

Figure 2.12 There are many different ways to check the feedback profile of an eBayer—just one click from here.

Are the Stars Out Tonight?

If you need (or want) to make a quick judgment about another eBayer, you can look at the color of the star that accompanies his or her name in the Feedback Profile (as well as many other eBay locations). Stars are awarded for achieving a particular number of positive responses.

▶   Yellow star: 10–99

▶   Turquoise star: 100–499

▶   Purple star: 500–999

▶   Red star: 1,000–9,999

▶   Shooting star: 10,000 or higher

Should you deal only with people who have high marks? Not necessarily. Read the specific feedback; a high total can mean many more positives than negatives as well as lots of positives. In addition, a new user might be a perfectly fine person, but not have been around long enough to get a star. The quality of his or her listing can provide other good evaluative information.

 Now I know how to check the feedback left about others. How I can leave feedback about other eBay users?

As you have seen with other feedback features, you do this through the Feedback Forum (See **Question 33**) as well. Just click on Leave Feedback and complete the form you see in **Figure 2.13**.

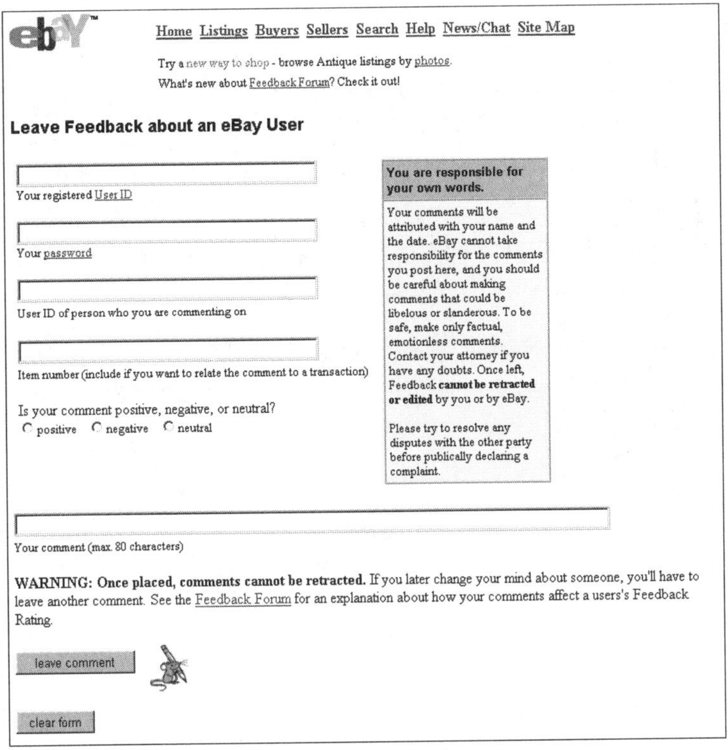

Figure 2.13 The form to use for leaving feedback about an eBay user.

Follow these steps to complete the form:

1. Enter your user ID.

2. Enter your password.

3. Enter the user ID of the eBay user about whom you wish to comment.

4. Enter the item number involved in the transaction.

5. Click whether your comment is positive (which means you had a good, smooth transaction), negative (which means you did not), or neutral (which means you are simply sharing information about your experience).

6. Enter your comment. It can be up to 80 characters long.

7. Click Leave Comment; your comment will appear as a part of that person's feedback.

A few things to remember about using feedback:

1. You can't leave feedback about yourself.

2. You own your words, so be sure this is something you want the entire eBay community to have access to—especially if your comment is negative. It can have a powerful affect on someone's transactions, to say nothing of the person's success as a buyer or seller. Be careful and be considerate. If you do make the error of leaving feedback that you later think is unfair, leave additional feedback trying to explain your lack of better planning.

3. No ranting or raving. You have 80 characters to say what you want, which should be more than enough to get your point across. Just say it and leave it.

4. Try to contact the seller to resolve what the disagreement is about before posting negative feedback. It's only right to give her a chance to respond to your allegations before the negative feedback is posted. This is particularly important because you will expect the same courtesy as you progress in the eBay community.

Negative Feedback: The Kiss of eBay Death

Everyone makes mistakes and that includes eBay buyers and sellers. The eBay community generally tolerates such errors. If negative feedback occurs repeatedly, however, that buyer or seller might be looking for a new auction home. If an eBayer receives a total of four negative feedbacks (a rating of −4), then that eBay user is automatically suspended from bidding, selling, or posting feedback—steps that prevent him from doing any damage to other eBay users. His status then goes through the SafeHarbor review to determine what future actions should be taken. SafeHarbor members communicate with the user and others involved and make the decision they think is best for the community. Everyone can live with you making one error—just don't make three more. The best way to keep all feedback positive is to keep in good touch through email with those you are buying from or selling to. It is fear of the unknown (no response from folks) that tends to increase negative feelings.

**What if I want to leave feedback about a particular item or sale transaction? Where and how can I do this?**

You can leave feedback for any reason that you want; just enter it in the Feedback Forum. Be sure to include the item number if you want to leave feedback about a particular eBay item. In eBay talk, this is called **transaction related feedback**. If you leave feedback that is unrelated to one particular item, you are leaving **non-transaction related feedback**.

Where can I find feedback that others have left about me?

Remember that golden rule? Feedback is a two way street, so if you leave feedback about other eBayers, you can bet that they will be leaving feedback about you. And in fact, when you have a transaction with a seller or a buyer, take the next step and leave feedback. Everyone in the eBay community benefits. One way eBay is better than the real world (besides the freedom to have cute user IDs) is that when customer service is good, you can immediately reward the seller with a big public thank you! The same goes for wanting to thank a particularly pleasant buyer. But be aware that if you leave negative feedback about someone, they might leave the same for you—whether justified or not!

You can see the feedback that people have left about you by clicking Review feedback on the Feedback Forum Web page. Once again, you need to type in your user ID and your password, click the number of comments you want to see and then click the button labeled view feedback.

How do I respond to feedback?

If you want to respond to feedback about you, click on the [env] button in the Feedback area. You will be able to leave a message for the individual who left feedback for you. Be truthful and direct.

Q39 Can I review the feedback that I have left for others?

You can see all the feedback that you have left about others by clicking on the Review feedback you have left about others link (on the Feedback Forum eBay page). You have to provide your user ID and your password and then click the button labeled List Feedback.

Q40 What does negative feedback look like?

Figure 2.14 shows you just a few of the hundreds of negative feedbacks this former eBayer accumulated before he was asked to leave. Not a pretty picture. You can read how the offenses range from not refunding money to not delivering items.

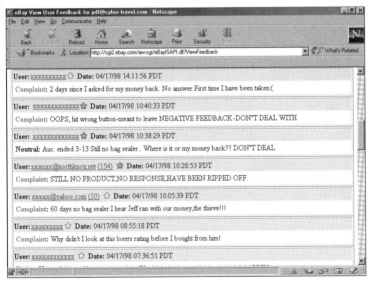

Figure 2.14 Not such nice feedback, right?

Another eBayer told me that feedback can be kept private. Why would I want to do that?

You can make all the feedback about your own eBay transactions private. This means that no one can access it (except you, of course). Before you do this, you should realize that if people have to regularly seek out feedback about you, it is sure to raise suspicions if that feedback isn't accessible— even if you have a good reason to make feedback about yourself private.

If you do want to make your feedback private, go to the Feedback Forum page and follow these steps:

1. Click Make Feedback Changes Public or Private.

2. Enter your user ID.

3. Enter your password.

4. Click Make My Feedback Profile Private if you want to do so. Click Make My Feedback Profile Public if that is the option you prefer. Note that this doesn't mean that others cannot leave feedback, just that it won't be readily accessible. Your feedback rating will still be shown to other users.

Look for Both Sellers and Buyers

Feedback strategies include verifying that the feedback was for selling the item, not for buying it. You have to look into the individual comments for this. Because many people do both, an impressively high rating might be due to buying a lot of stuff; the person may have little experience selling items and may not be good at communicating, packaging, mailing on time, or accurately describing items. From a community standpoint, someone who has done both selling and buying is trustworthy. They are more a part of the community, not just a user of the community.

My Internet Service Provider went out of business and I had to change my email address. How can I be sure that all my great feedback follows me?

eBay will make sure that your new email address will replace your old email address and that your new address is associated with your feedback, buying and selling, and any other eBay activity that includes your user ID.

eBay, however, prefers you not register your new email address until you have first completed the Change of Email Address form. After you change your email address and register the new one, the old and new email addresses will be merged and your eBay records will reflect the change.

To change your email address, follow these steps:

1. Click on the site map link at the top of any eBay page.

2. Click Change Email Address (located under Registered User Services).

3. Provide your user ID, password, and new email address.

4. Click on the button labeled Submit.

By the way, eBay does not like mixing uppercase or capital letters, so enter the email address and password using lowercase letters.

Feedback: Good, but Not Perfect

No matter how attentive you are or what efforts eBay might make, buyers and sellers can still be cheated. One crook operated this way. He built up a feedback rating of 200 or 300, then placed several items in the Featured Items section with prices too good to be true. Lots of eBayers wanted the good deal and sent in their money, only to find their mailboxes empty of goods they paid for. This seller never shipped anything, made thousands of dollars, and even eBay had a hard time tracking him down because he changed email addresses and user IDs so often. It's very hard for anyone to fight this kind of theft—but perhaps better judgment up front should be used. If an eBay item seems priced far below market value and there's no obvious reason why, it's a good idea to look elsewhere. Another caveat is to see if a reserve price exists (See **Question 53**) on these low minimum bid items. A legitimate seller might offer a valuable item at a $1.00 minimum bid just to make things exciting, but may try and protect themselves with a reserve price (or a minimum price they will take of the item). A low minimum without a reserve price for a really valuable item doesn't always mean the seller is trouble, it might mean that he loves to gamble.

Bidding Basics

 **I found what I want to bid on and checked out the seller. How do I bid?**

This is the real moment of truth and one that we bet you've been excited about since you first learned what eBay is all about.

Bidding involves some very simple steps:

1. Find the item on which you want to bid.
2. Click on the item listing so you can see the complete item description.
3. Place your bid.
4. Confirm your bid.

Let's go through the steps as we actually search for a copy of Tom Clancy's first book, *The Hunt for Red October*.

Find the Item You Want

This is more or less a cinch. Enter the words *The Hunt for Red October* in any Search box and click the

Search

button. eBay does its thing and provides 18 items that contain these words (**Figure 2.15**). As you have seen, each item contains the item number (such as 71420644), the online listing (Tom Clancy The Hunt For Red October Nice!), the latest price bid ($10.50), the number of bids (2), and the auction's ending date and time (03/4 18:25).

Figure 2.15 The results of our *The Hunt for Red October* simple search.

See the Complete Item Description

Click on the single-line listing and then plan on spending lots of time reading about the item you are considering for a bid. As you can see in **Figure 2.16**, the complete item description is full of interesting and useful information. The complete item description is separate from the bidding section, which begins about halfway down that same page. We get to that momentarily.

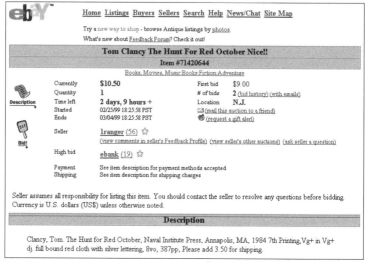

Home Listings Buyers Sellers Search Help News/Chat Site Map

Try a new way to shop - browse Antique listings by photos.
What's new about Feedback Forum? Check it out!

Tom Clancy The Hunt For Red October Nice!!
Item #71420644

Books, Movies, Music:Books:Fiction:Adventure

Description	Currently	**$10.50**	First bid	$9.00
	Quantity	1	# of bids	2 (bid history) (with emails)
	Time left	**2 days, 9 hours +**	Location	**N.J.**
	Started	02/25/99 18:25:58 PST	(mail this auction to a friend)	
	Ends	03/04/99 18:25:58 PST	(request a gift alert)	
Bid!	Seller	1ranger (56) ☆		
		(view comments in seller's Feedback Profile) (view seller's other auctions) (ask seller a question)		
	High bid	ebank (19) ☆		
	Payment	See item description for payment methods accepted		
	Shipping	See item description for shipping charges		

Seller assumes all responsibility for listing this item. You should contact the seller to resolve any questions before bidding.
Currency is U.S. dollars (US$) unless otherwise noted.

Description

Clancy, Tom. The Hunt for Red October, Naval Institute Press, Annapolis, MA, 1984 7th Printing,Vg+ in Vg+ dj. full bound red cloth with silver lettering, 8vo, 387pp, Please add 3.50 for shipping.

Figure 2.16 A typical item description.

Let's first go through the top half of the page and tackle the major things. We get to more of the fun stuff after that.

► At the top of the page you see the title of the item and underneath that the item number.

► The high bid for this item is currently $10.50. The first bid was $9.00.

► There is only one of these available (Quantity 1) and there have already been two bids.

► There are two days and nine hours left in the auction and the bidder is in New Jersey. Bidder location gives you a sense of what the postage might be.

► The auction started on 2/25/99 at 18:25.58 (about 6 P.M. Pacific Coast Time) and ends on 3/4/99 at the same time. This auction runs for seven days.

► The seller's and the high bidder's User ID's are both listed.

► There's information about how the seller wants to be paid at the bottom of the page.

► There's a brief written description of the item itself. In many cases, there will be a picture accompanying the item that follows this written description.

You should make sure of these things: are you completely satisfied with what you see; do you agree with all the terms set forth in the user agreement (when you registered); are you in agreement with the payment and shipping terms the seller has stated; do you want to bid? If so, go for it.

Place Your Bid

Click on the bid icon (or simply scroll down); you are taken to the bidding section of the Item Description page as shown in **Figure 2.17**.

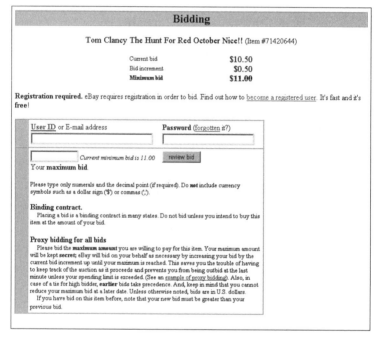

Figure 2.17 This is the Bidding location.

Now follow these steps:

1. Enter your user ID. If you forgot it or don't have one, use your email address.

2. Enter your password. If you forgot it, click on the Forgotten It? link. eBay will send you instructions for getting back on track.

3. Enter your maximum bid, which in this case must be at least $11.00. There's no harm in entering a bid amount that is less than the current bid; eBay will simply let you know that you have made a mistake. eBay keeps track of what the minimum bid should be and keeps you on track as well!

4. Click the button labeled Review Bid.

Confirm Your Bid

You should see a summary of your proposed bid (**Figure 2.18**) in addition to other important information, including an invitation for you to check the seller's feedback. This is an essential step in the buying process. As discussed earlier, click on both the number of feedbacks as well as a description of the feedback rating system to get both comments and a summary.

    Home Listings Buyers Sellers Search Help News/Chat Site Map

Try a new way to shop - browse Antique listings by photos.
What's new about Feedback Forum? Check it out!

Review bid for: Tom Clancy The Hunt For Red October Nice!! (item #71420644)

Your bid was in the amount of: **$11.00**
Your maximum bid was in the amount of: **$15.00**
The User ID you entered was: **neiljsalkind**

Before finalizing your bid:

1. View comments left by other users in the Feedback Profile for the seller: 1ranger (56) ☆

2. Be sure you understand the seller's payment and shipping terms and conditions. Your bid means that you accept them and will comply if you are the winning bidder.

3. For expensive items, consider using safe, easy-to-use escrow services to make sure that you get what you pay for. Two services to consider are i-Escrow and TradeSafe.

If your bid amount is correct, click the 'place bid' button below. Otherwise, use the back button on your browser to go back and make the necessary corrections. **Once you place your bid, you cannot cancel it.**

    place bid

    Click here if you wish to cancel

Figure 2.18 Reviewing and getting ready to confirm a bid.

When you are confident that you want to purchase this item at the price you bid and are satisfied that the seller is reliable, click the Place Bid button.

When you click that button, you have agreed to several things:

▶ You intend to buy what you bid on at the price you entered. It's unlikely that anyone would take any legal action against you if you were the high bidder and refused to follow through, but it sure isn't the right thing to do. It also would almost guarantee negative feedback.

▶ This bid is fixed and you cannot lower it.

One of two things happens when you place that bid. Either you become the current high bidder and eBay congratulates you (**Figure 2.19**), or eBay tells you that you have been outbid by another bidder.

Bid confirmed for: Tom Clancy The Hunt For Red October Nice!! (item #71420644)

```
Your bid was in the amount of:        $11.00
Your maximum bid was in the amount of: $15.00
After processing all the open bids for
this item, the current bid price is   $11.00
```

Thank you for your bid! **You** are the current **high bidder** for this item! You will be notified if your maximum bid is exceeded by another bidder.

Figure 2.19 A bid confirmation.

How in the world can you be outbid when you just bid more than the highest bid? Easily. An earlier bidder outbid you by specifying a higher maximum than you were willing to bid. Simply, someone bid that maximum before you did and when your bid was entered, eBay automatically ensured that the highest bid was entered. This is the eBay **proxy system** at work, insuring that no one artificially pumps up the price of an item.

Speak Your Peace!

Sometimes it's a good idea to contact the seller with any questions that you might have before you bid. For example, you might have required shipping instructions (the item must be sent FedEx, not UPS or postal mail) or you might want the item to be shipped to another address since it's a gift that you want kept secret.

The key is to ask the seller about such arrangements before you bid, so you can be sure that the special arrangements are possible and so you're not caught short after the bidding stops and you've won the auction. You can ask the seller any relevant question about the item: more details about condition, what the reserve price is, or if other similar items are available. You can contact the seller by clicking on his or her user ID anywhere in eBay.

There are all kinds of information on the Item Description page. What can I do with it?

There are indeed some nice tricks that you can perform from this page. For example, clicking on the Mail This Auction to a Friend Link

allows you to send the auction to a friend, which is sneaky way of telling your friend, "Wow, would it be cool if you got this for me!"

The Request a Gift Alert link allows you to notify a friend that you have purchased a gift on eBay for him or her. How sweet! The note that goes to your buddy is shown in **Figure 2.20** and is lots of fun.

A Gift For You!

to
Mom

(Click on the wrapped gift to open it!)

from
Your Loving Daughter

Figure 2.20 How cute—a gift is on its way to you.

How Cool Is This?
Mary loved the diamond ring that she saw on eBay and knew that she and her boyfriend had talked about what a nice gift a ring would make. Rather than dropping hints over dinner and on the way to work, she emailed him a gift alert. He took the hint and on Valentine's Day, there was the ring on her pillow. True story!

Q45 How much should I offer as my first bid?

This is usually the first question that bidders think about, whether this is the first or fortieth auction that they are participating in. To assure that you are in a position to get the item you are bidding on, bid the amount that you think the item is worth and the maximum you can afford.

You should only bid what you think an item is worth (regardless of what other people may think or bid), since you only want to pay what you think is a fair market value. If you bid more and end up as the high bidder, you'll feel cheated.

If you bid the maximum you can afford, you won't put yourself in danger of having to retract your bid from overbidding. You won't position yourself to exceed by proxy many of the bids that will be made as the price of the item is bid up during the auction.

If you enjoy sitting in front of your computer and reloading your browser and watching your precious item's price increase every 10 minutes, that's fine. If you want to place a bid that you think is fair and then let eBay do the rest, the proxy mechanism is available. Remember that one of eBay's standard procedures is to notify you via email.

Buy Now or Later?

There's not really ever a rush to bid until the last few hours, and even then you have time. Why not wait a day or two to verify that you really, really want the item? One can get caught up in the excitement of seeing an obscure item listed. Enjoy just seeing the listing. Read the description carefully. Look at the image carefully. Read the feedback about the seller. See what other items the seller has up for auction. Get a sense of whether he is a collector, dealer, hobbyist, amateur, or professional.

Do you still want it? If so, make sure you are done browsing or searching before you bid. You might find the same item in better shape right after you've committed a bid on a poorer quality copy. You might find a better "perfect gift" for someone you wish you now could bid on. Avoid impulse bidding, and use eBay responsibly!

Q46 How much should I bid?

This is a more profound question than you might think. The simple answer is to bid as much as you are willing to pay for the item. How much are you really willing to pay? We recommend this series of psychologically tested and approved steps:

1. When you find an item that you simply must have, don't immediately click on the Bid button. Unless there are only minutes remaining in the auction, what's the hurry? Take a deep breath and think. Is it the idea that an interesting item is available that most excites you, or do you actually want to own it?

2. To decide how much to bid, consider first what you can afford to spend on this sort of thing. This becomes your upper limit. Don't bid more than that—even if the bidding gets exciting and you could win if you bid just $2.00 more! There will be other auctions and you will live to fight again.

3. Having decided on your maximum bid based on what you can afford, lower your maximum bid to the exact amount (to the penny) that reflects exactly how much you want this item. This is a tough skill to develop, but is a fun cognitive exercise. Imagine you want the item for $22.00. Would you want it for $22.01? If yes, then the real maximum bid you want is $22.01, not $22.00. How about $22.02? At what point in this price adjustment do you lose interest? Learn to find that magic amount and you will always be happy when you win an auction. As a bidding strategy, adding that extra penny can make the difference between winning and losing. Most bidders' maximum bid is a nice round figure. Your extra penny could make you the high bidder.

4. Before entering your maximum bid, remind yourself that there will be mailing and packaging costs. That's real money out of your pocket, so you should count that as part of your cost for the item.

Q47 What is proxy bidding and how is it used?

Proxy bidding is just another name for the automatic bidding described earlier. There's no real person bidding; eBay automatically acts as a proxy for the highest bidder to assure that the auction moves ahead. When you place a bid that is high enough to outbid any other, eBay acts as your proxy to assure that your position in the bidding process is protected. eBay acts as the bidder's representative and continues to bid as necessary until the auction either ends, and the item is won, or someone else bids more than their maximum amount and the item is lost. See the term proxy bidding in the Glossary for more information.

Q48 What happens if I am the highest bidder and the bid is accepted?

One of eBay's most important jobs is to keep its bidders (and sellers) appraised of what's happening with the items they are bidding on and selling. When you make a bid, eBay automatically notifies you that your bid has been accepted and confirmed and entered into the system. It is our experience that these messages are sent immediately after the system accepts your bid, but there can be delays if eBay is especially busy, such as around holiday time. In **Figure 2.21** you can see what a high bidder message looks like.

Home **Listings** **Buyers** **Sellers** **Search** **Help** News/Chat **Site Map**

Protect yourself from listing or buying <u>illegal or infringing</u> items.

Manage all your transactions in one place -- <u>My eBay</u>, the best kept secret on eBay.

Bid confirmed for: Nicholson Baker's ROOM TEMPERATURE. (item #84734280)

```
Your bid was in the amount of:        $5.50
Your maximum bid was in the amount of: $6.00
After processing all the open bids for
this item, the current bid price is   $5.00
```

Thank you for your bid! **You** are the current **high bidder** for this item! You will be notified if your maximum bid is exceeded by another bidder.

Please note that the listings on the index pages are not updated right away, but your bid has been recorded.

Important: please take note of the closing date of this auction. At midnight following the close, the seller and the high-bidder will be notified by e-mail, and you have only **three** business days to contact each other before losing your position as high-bidder.

Figure 2.21 The confirmation from eBay that you are the high bidder.

The eBay message tells you everything you need to know about the ongoing auction where you were the high bidder, including the amount of the bid, when the auction closes, and the eBay address you can click and go to the item. You receive a notice if you are ever outbid. Additionally, you receive a daily update of your auction status. Bidders only receive these daily updates as long as they are a high bidder in any auction. Sellers who are offering items at auctions receive a daily update until the auctions are over. All these notices are designed for you, so you don't have to log on constantly to check your status. All you have to do is check your email.

Q49 What happens if I am outbid?

Good question. For one thing, you're no longer in the running for the item and you'll know it when eBay sends you an email message telling you so. You can either withdraw from the auction (which requires no action on your part) or click on the Web link in the notifying email message, go back, and bid again. Should you go back and bid again? It depends upon how much you want the item and what you are willing to spend. It's all your decision, but just don't get into a contest with another bidder to see who can bid the most!

Q50   How do I know when an auction ends?

An auction ends when the time it was slated for expires; this is always three, five, or seven days (and 14 days during the Christmas holidays) after it started. You can tell when the auction for a particular item will end; that information is available on the complete item description. Once the time has passed, a bright red Auction Ended message appears in the item description. Best of all, if you are high bidder you get an email notice from eBay telling you that the auction has ended. Another way to check on your status across all auctions is via My eBay (See **Question 56**).

The results of an auction are available up to 30 days after the auction ends. You can always see the final auction history, including who won and what price the item sold at, as well as the **bidding history** (a list of what bid amounts were made along the way), which is almost always kept secret while an auction is in progress. If you want to return to that auction's page, click the Search icon at the top of the eBay home page; enter the item number in the Item Lookup box and click the Look Up button. You can also search by the name of the item using the Title Search box. Additionally, you may still have the item's location in one of the emails you received during the auction.

Q51

What happens once the auction ends?

Shortly after the auction closes and the item is yours, you should receive an email from eBay indicating that you have won the auction. You should shortly thereafter get a message from the seller and instructions regarding how to get the item you bid on. In general, these instructions will recap what item was sold and bought, the closing price, and the shipping instructions. There should be no surprises.

Then there's the fine print. There may be special instructions from the seller, so read these notices very carefully. For example, you might be asked to notify the seller within five days via email to be sure that you got the notice about your winning the auction and then payment must arrive within 10 days. It just depends upon the seller's wishes. At the very least, a good seller should let you know what item you won and the total amount due with postage.

Real Special Wishes

A one-of-a-kind Mickey Mouse drawing was being recently offered on eBay for $925,000.00 (a lot of cheese for a piece of art that probably wasn't even in color) and the shipping instructions were quite complex. Only serious buyers were asked to bid and if the item was sold (the auction ended with no bids, however), the buyer was to wire 10% of the cost (about $100,000.00 smackeroos) to the seller's escrow account in care of the seller's attorney in New York City. For an item of this value, the buyer and seller would have certainly been in close contact.

Look for other special notes or requests from the seller. In one case, the seller had difficulty getting his U.S. Postal Mail delivered reliably and asked the buyer to print very clearly the seller's name and address on the envelope containing payment. If the seller accepts credit cards, you may be asked to call or visit a secure server to pay for your item.

There are too many possibilities to list. Just be aware that you should spend some time reading the confirmation notice about your winning bid and following the instructions as carefully as you can. If you have any questions about payment or shipping arrangements, contact the seller via email. The easiest way to do this is to click on the Ask Seller a Question link (located below the seller's user ID on the Item Description page).

If you don't hear from the seller within a few days, it is time to try and contact him or her again. Since you are a registered user, as is the seller, you can ask eBay to contact both parties and help make the connection. Here's how to do that:

To use eBay to make contact with another registered user (through eBay and not through direct email), follow three steps.

1. Click on the site map at the top of any eBay Web page.

2. Click the Contact Other Registered User link (located under Registered User Services).

3. Fill in your user ID and password, as well as the other person's user ID; click Send Request.

eBay will make every effort to get you connected and talking. You should both receive notification that someone is trying to get in contact and instructions for how to do that.

Q52

Is there any way I can learn some of the other bids placed on an item?

You can, but only after the auction has ended and you can look at the history. For example, a completed auction is shown in **Figure 2.22**. You can see the last bid for the item, who the seller was, what the first bid was, and the number of bids made. Most interesting? The amounts bid. You can see a history of those amounts and the biding increments in the lower section of Figure 2.22. Of course, you can identify the person who did the bidding and look at their feedback as well.

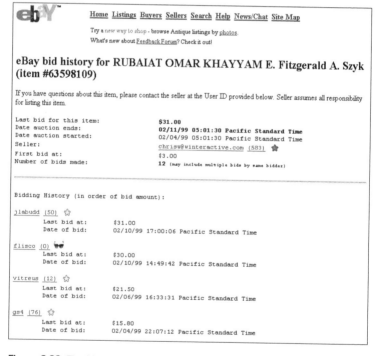

eBay bid history for RUBAIAT OMAR KHAYYAM E. Fitzgerald A. Szyk (item #63598109)

Home Listings Buyers Sellers Search Help News/Chat Site Map

Try a new way to shop - browse Antique listings by photos.
What's new about Feedback Forum? Check it out!

If you have questions about this item, please contact the seller at the User ID provided below. Seller assumes all responsibility for listing this item.

Last bid for this item: $31.00
Date auction ends: 02/11/99 05:01:30 Pacific Standard Time
Date auction started: 02/04/99 05:01:30 Pacific Standard Time
Seller: chrisw@winteractive.com (583)
First bid at: $3.00
Number of bids made: 12 (may include multiple bids by same bidder)

Bidding History (in order of bid amount):

jlabudd (50)
    Last bid at: $31.00
    Date of bid: 02/10/99 17:00:06 Pacific Standard Time

flisco (0)
    Last bid at: $30.00
    Date of bid: 02/10/99 14:49:42 Pacific Standard Time

vitreus (12)
    Last bid at: $21.50
    Date of bid: 02/06/99 16:33:31 Pacific Standard Time

gs4 (76)
    Last bid at: $15.80
    Date of bid: 02/04/99 22:07:12 Pacific Standard Time

Figure 2.22 The history of bids on an item after the auction has ended.

Why would you want to see the bidding history? It's a great way to better understand an eBayer's general approach to bidding and make you a more successful, sharper bidder.

"I learned that if you bid on too many things at the same time your e-mail becomes flooded and it is very confusing to know what you have rebid on or what email was answered unless you make a list. You have to save a lot of messages until you get an address to send payment to. Put the absolute highest price you'd ever pay the first time. That way you don't have to rebid, you can just delete it. Narrow the search field or you get 3,000 responses (i.e.: don't enter goalie, but put goalie pads)."

—Mary from Nebraska

 I made a bid, but noticed that it was a reserve price auction. What is a reserve auction and how does it work?

eBay auctions always start at a particular value (set by the seller) such as $10.00 and the bid increment is defined by eBay depending upon the price of the item and the starting point (so a new bid can be automatically entered on the bidding portion of the Item Description page). Bidding takes place and the highest bidder wins, regardless of the price. This is a good, old-fashioned, regular auction and doesn't have a special name.

A **reserve price auction** (also called a **reserve auction**) is where the seller sets a particular price below which the item will not be sold. In other words, it's the lowest possible price that an item will sell for. If the seller sets a price of $25.00 and the highest bid is $24.50, the seller is not obligated to sell the item to that highest bidder. Make sure that when you first read through the complete item description, you notice whether this is a reserve (or some other type of) auction. If you bid and think you have an item because you are the high bidder, but haven't yet exceeded the reserve and are unaware that you are required to do so, you are likely to be upset.

How do you know when an auction is a reserve auction? The item description says so next to the item reserve amount: Reserve Not Yet Met (**Figure 2.23**). In this case, it means that the current bid of $7000.00 has yet to meet the reserve price the seller set prior to opening the auction.

A REAL Nicolaus Gagliano VIOLIN!		
Item #69328614		
Miscellaneous:Musical Instruments:String		
Currently	$7000.00 (reserve not yet met) ❶	First bid $2500.00

❶ Here's the indication this is a reserve auction.

Figure 2.23 Look for the little comment that shows you this is a reserve auction.

How can you tell what the reserve price is? You can't. That would render this type of auction. The other value for the seller of a reserve auction is that if no bid meets the reserve price, the seller at least has a sense of what the true free market value for the item might be. High but unsuccessful bidders often receive email from the reserve auction seller, letting them know what the reserve was and offering to negotiate a price acceptable to both. By the way, if the sale of an item resulted from its appearance on eBay, we think the seller owes eBay a cut. And, eBay does not allow the seller to change from Reserve to a regular auction once Reserve has been selected.

Q54 What are the other types of auctions?

There are several kinds of auctions. We have already gone through the basic and the reserve price auctions. Now let's talk about three other types of auctions: Dutch, private, and restricted access.

A **Dutch auction** is one in which a seller has more than one identical item to sell. The seller sets a minimum price and the number of items that are available; you can see that information on the Item Description screen. When the auction ends, the individual bidder who made the highest bid (above the minimum set by the seller) can purchase as many items as specified. That buyer may not have to pay the high bid amount, however. If not all the items were bid on at that price, buyers pay the lowest bid amount that claimed the last of the items for sale.

For example, say that a seller has available 200 pens, with a high bid of $10.00. If 250 eBayers wanted one pen and bid on this item at the $10.00 amount, only the first 200 would be winners and each would get 1 pen. The last 50 to bid would not get one at all since their bids were submitted later than the first 200. You can make bids on more than one of the items as well, but if you are outbid, you may not end up with any or even all of the items you want. On the other hand, if one person bid $10.50 on the pen, only wanted 1, and 50 other bidders only bid $10.00, that first bidder would only have to pay the lowest successful bid of $10.00. Dutch auctions determine a fair price because it is directly based on supply and demand.

A **private auction** is an auction well described by its title—no one knows who bids because the bidder's email address is not shown on the screen, nor is it publicly available. The only two people who are notified about the sale are the buyer and the seller (once the auction has ended).

Restricted access auctions were created by eBay so that particular areas of eBay were not as easily accessible as others. Right now, there's only the Erotica, Adult-Only site that is restricted. (Firearms used to be restricted, but is no longer a category.) In order to visit the adult site, you need a credit card number on file with eBay. It's the best way they have of checking whether someone is over 18 years of age.

Section 2   Buying

Oops! I Wanted to Bid $50.00, Not $500.00 Dollars!

You can retract a bid if you made an honest mistake on a bid and have a reasonable explanation. This should be a last and dramatic step and should not be taken lightly. What reasons are acceptable for retracting a bid?

▶ Typographical errors (such as $500.00 rather than $50.00)

▶ The description of the item has changed after you made you bid

▶ A personal or medical emergency prevents you from continuing

Retractions are not private. Retractions become public knowledge in the bidding history and you might be asked via email to explain your actions. To retract a bid, follow these steps:

1. From the site map, click on Retract a Bid Under Bidding Management.

2. Enter your user ID, your password, and the item number of the auction for which you want all your bids retracted.

3. Enter you explanation. The form only allows 80 characters, so you don't have much room. Be concise and precise.

4. Click the Retract Bid button and your bid is retracted. Although eBay claims that it is reviewed, the approval happens so fast that such retractions are, more or less, automatic.

It would be polite to send an email to the seller and tell him why you had to retract your bid. It saves him wondering and having to ask you—which he probably will do.

If retraction is successful, all the bids you placed in an auction are deleted. If you make a typo and enter the wrong bid value and then retract another bid, you'll have to bid again. Note that while you can retract a bid, you cannot change an existing bid's value. An exception, of sorts, is that you can always increase your maximum bid, even if you are currently the high bidder. This procedure tells eBay to keep in mind that you are now willing to pay more if necessary, but does not increase your current high bid.

 ### Are there special tools that I can use to help me get the item I want?

There are all kinds of helpers that do things such as show you every minute of your bid status and allow you to track all of your eBay activity. The two best, The Watcher and The Feedback Wizard are reviewed in Appendix A, "Need Help?"

Keeping Track

 ### There must be a special way to keep track of all my activities. Is there a way to personalize my eBay activities?

My eBay is the answer to keeping everything in its place. As you can see in **Figure 2.24**, this eBay helper lists your favorite areas of eBay, feedback, information about your account, and information about items that you are selling and buying. To create a My eBay page, follow these instructions:

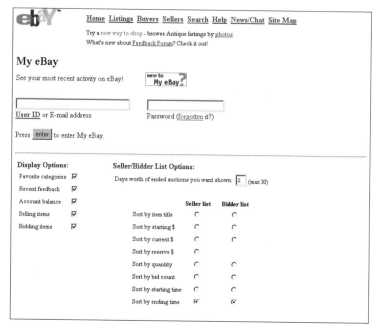

Figure 2.24 Creating your own My eBay to include special information and formatting.

1. Click on the site map link at the top of any eBay Web page.

2. Click My eBay (located under Item Management). You will see the form shown in Figure 2.24.

3. Enter your user ID.

4. Enter your password.

5. Select what you want displayed. This can include your favorite categories, recent feedback, account balance (See **Question 69**), items that you are selling, and items that you are buying.

6. Insert a number that represents the number of days for which you want ended auctions shown.

7. Specify how you want selling and bidding items sorted.

8. Click Enter; you're on your way. The next thing you'll see (**Figure 2.25**) is a nice summary of your activity.

Home Listings Buyers Sellers Search Help News/Chat Site Map

Protect yourself from listing or buying illegal or infringing items.

Check out March's eBay Life, your community newsletter.

My eBay!

neiljsalkind

My Feedback (5)

Recent feedback about me:

03/02/99   eslone (eslone@scs-intl.com) (287) ⭐ (praise)
12:19:41   Rapid response and payment, what more could you ask for!!

01/21/99   gewel@worldnet.att.net (223) ⭐ (praise)
01:52:16   Excellent Transaction, Fast Payment, Great Emails. Recommended!

12/23/98   julianbook@aol.com (312) ⭐ (praise)
17:59:07   Fantastic eBay user - highest recommendation - thanks.

See all feedback about me
Review and respond to feedback about me
See all feedback I have left about others

My Account

As of **03/04/99 09:45:36**, my account balance is: **9.50**

Full account status: last 2 months only - entire account (this might take a while; please be patient)
Up to the minute accounting of all credits, debits and current balance for your eBay accounts. Accounts are not created until the first credit or debit is posted, so even if you have already created your account, no information will be here until the first account activity.

Fees & credits - Payment terms - Use a credit card for automatic billing - Credit request - Refunds - Make a one time payment

Items I'm Selling

See details...

Item	Start $	Current $	Reserve $	Quant	Bids	Start	End PST	Time Left
Nice Ten Commandments illustrated by Szyk (reserve not yet met)								
73979187	5.00	12.30	20.00	1	3	03/04	03/11 08:46	2d 21h 29m

Red indicates items that would not sell if the auction were to end now.
Green indicates items that would sell if the auction were to end now.
Click on an underlined column heading to sort in either ascending or descending order.

Add an item - Tips for sellers - FAQ - After the auction

Items I'm Bidding On

See details...

Item	Start $	Current $	My Max $	Quant	Bids	Start	End PST	Time Left
1947 JEWISH BOOK of RUTH-ARTHUR SZYK-Judaica								
72911637	85.00	94.38	95.00	1 of 1	4	03/01	03/08 16:14	0d 4h 57m
SILVER SZYK Illus. Passover Haggadah, Judaica								
74143702	1.99	107.50	125.00	1 of 1	15	03/04	03/11 17:00	3d 5h 43m

Red indicates auctions in which you are not currently winning.
Green indicates auctions in which you are currently winning.
Note: Dutch auctions do not use the color coding.
Click on an underlined column heading to sort in either ascending or descending order.

Search - Wanted page - Tips for buyers - FAQ - After the auction

 Home Listings Buyers Sellers Search Help News/Chat Site Map

Thank you for using eBay!

About eBay | SafeHarbor

Figure 2.25 A typical My eBay page complete with information about everything from feedback to bidding and selling activity.

Section 2 Buying

After the Bid

I won the auction and the item I wanted is mine! How do I get it?

You and the seller should have exchanged emails, you're verifying that you are going to pay, and the seller is providing you with information about payment and shipping costs and such.

Sellers often provide several alternatives for both payment and shipping. For the most part, sellers want to get paid in a safe and expedient manner, which usually means paying them using a cashier's or bank check or money order. None of these need to be verified (they are like cash in that manner). Many sellers, especially small businesses, are accepting credit cards, an easy form of payment to verify. Some sellers now even offer secure servers on which credit card numbers can be sent and used for payment. If you do pay by personal check, you can expect the seller to wait until the check **clears** (when the bank verifies that sufficient money is in your account to cover the amount of the check) before the item is sent off. This should take fewer than 10 business days from the deposit of your check, so be patient.

Sellers often offer various shipping options, which can include regular U.S. Mail, priority services, or UPS. There are costs associated with all of these, so be sure to read the note from the seller carefully before sending payment; ensure that you're sending the correct amount.

It is the responsibility of both the seller and the buyer to reach a mutually satisfactory arrangement for payment and shipping. The vast majority of eBay transactions are smooth and easy to complete.

I just got what I bid on and it's not what I want. Is there anything I can do?

Most eBayers are in for the long haul, meaning that the last thing they want is to spoil their feedback, disappoint their buyers, or endanger their relationship with other eBayers. If you find that what you got is not exactly what you expected or the item is unsatisfactory and want to return it, consider the following:

▶ Don't send the item back without first contacting the seller. This provides an opportunity for you and the seller to discuss the nature of the complaint and maybe work things out without having to return the item to the seller at all. Try email first. If need be, you can get user contact information and try regular mail and telephone to resolve the dispute.

▶ Try to keep lines of communication open all the time. You can bring eBay into the fray if you want (although they will be very reluctant to mediate any dispute), but better you settle things directly and get on with your eBay activities.

▶ Time is of the essence. Once you send off your payment, you should expect to receive your item within two weeks. If you have any questions or objections, you are expected to contact the buyer immediately after receiving and examining your item.

▶ If the unlikely happens, and things do not end satisfactorily for you, certainly leave negative feedback about the seller. Of course, the seller may have another perspective and be leaving some feedback of their own. The huge majority of eBay transactions, however, are positive, happy experiences which is why the huge majority of eBayers have good feedback ratings.

eBay—More addictive than chocolate!

"I have just recently begun bidding on auctions and I love it! I am addicted to it and my friends think I'm nuts. Of course, they are the ones that haven't tried it yet. My tip for new users is to find an item they like and then click on Seller's Other Auctions. This way, they know that they are dealing with someone who has some good stuff or they wouldn't have bid in the first place and, the more you buy from the same person, the cheaper the shipping costs will be. I've found that to be a lifesaver!

—Sallie from Indianapolis

 I just won the auction for a 1998 Harley Davidson Heritage Springer motorcycle for $16,500.00 and I just can't see sending a check or money order for that large an amount. Isn't there a safer way to exchange my money for what I bought so I can be sure I'm getting what I paid for?

What you want is some kind of an escrow service where the seller and buyer have the item and the money (in whatever form) held by a third party until both the buyer and the seller are satisfied.

eBay recommends two escrow services. TradeSafe (**www.tradesafe.com**) and i-Escrow (**www.i-Escrow.com**), which work in generally the same way:

1. The buyer, the seller, and the escrow agent agree to do business. In some cases the seller pays the shipping costs of the item and the buyer pays the escrow agent's fee.

2. A form is completed, including information about the buyer and the seller and the details of the transaction.

3. The buyer sends in payment to the escrow agent using a personal check, a money order, bank check, credit card, or wire transfer. The buyer has a short period of time to complete this part of the transaction. Once the funds have been received and have cleared, the seller will be notified to ship the goods.

4. The seller ships the good to the buyer.

5. The buyer receives the goods and inspects them immediately. If they are not acceptable, the escrow agent is contacted and withholds payment to the seller. From there, the buyer and seller need to resolve any conflict.

How much does this cost? About 2%–5% of the purchase price, depending upon the escrow agent and the cost of the item. For a $1,200.00 item, the fee could be about $45.00. For your motorcycle described, it would about $600.00.

Is it worth using an escrow agent? That depends almost entirely on how much trust you have in the seller you are dealing with. If the feedback is great and you have dealt with this seller before, you probably have little cause for concern. On the other hand, if you are dealing with someone for the first time, feedback is limited or questionable, and it's a big sale for you, we suggest using one of these services. For these large sales, it seems prudent to always have spoken to the seller at least over the phone, not just through email.

Section 2 Buying

Going Global

 **I heard that I can now bid and sell across borders. How do I do that?**

eBay has items available to bid on from over 50 countries, so you are certainly not limited by your own national borders. You do just about everything else the same way as if you were bidding to buy an item from a friend who lived across the street.

Except customs. You just can't go shipping anything across borders and in addition, there are duties and taxes and other fees that might come due—usually to be paid by the buyer. Then there are regulations both by the shipping country (mostly the U.S.) and the country in which the person who is receiving the item lives that need to be adhered to. For example, there are specific limitations on sending high-technology equipment to certain Eastern countries. At best, while you can bid on items listed from foreign countries, be sure to spend extra time investigating the implications of such activity. eBay has a nice link to information about customs around the world. You can find the information at **http://www.wcoomd.org/frmpublic.htm.table.**

Section 3
Selling

Selling

Selling

Selling

Selling

elling

3

Selling

Have you ever heard that one person's trash is another person's treasure? That's what keeps eBay as popular as it is. People who are cleaning out their attics, basements, and storerooms; others who have worked years at establishing collections; these people offer their items in good faith to the highest bidder. That's where the trash and treasure thing comes in. With millions of items on eBay and hundreds of thousands of buyers, there's always a market.

How do you create an auction? What about those fancy pictures in item descriptions? What should I charge? How much does eBay charge? Why does "Gee, I'll quit my job and sell Froibles on eBay!" sound good, but require so much planning? That and more is what we'll cover in this last important section of *eBay Online Auctions.*

Getting Started Selling

How do I get started listing an item for auction?

If you thought buying was fun, hang around. This is where eBay gets really addictive.

You know that set of lead soldiers that have been in the top drawer of your old dresser for 25 years? Somebody would love that and would probably pay well for it. What about those old comic books? They don't need to be mint; someone wants them. That set of Doc Savage paperback novels? Put those on the block as well.

Selling is great fun, not only because of the money you can earn, but the simple activity of watching the bids go up and up. If you're ambitious enough, like thousands of other eBayers, you might find a career as a full-time eBayer too much to resist.

How to get started? Easy. Selling items on eBay consists of three steps:

1. Starting an auction and listing your items for sale.

2. Verify your entry to be sure that the information (from the item description to the starting bid to the reserve price) is correct.

3. View the confirmation that your auction has started.

Let's go through these step by step as we put up a book for sale.

Listing Your Item

The selling process begins with the completion of the form you see in **Figure 3.1**. To get to this form, click on the graphic found on the eBay home page. So you can see what it looks like when completed, we've already entered the necessary information to sell a book by Arthur Szyk, a famous illustrator.

1. Enter your user ID or email address.

2. Enter your password.

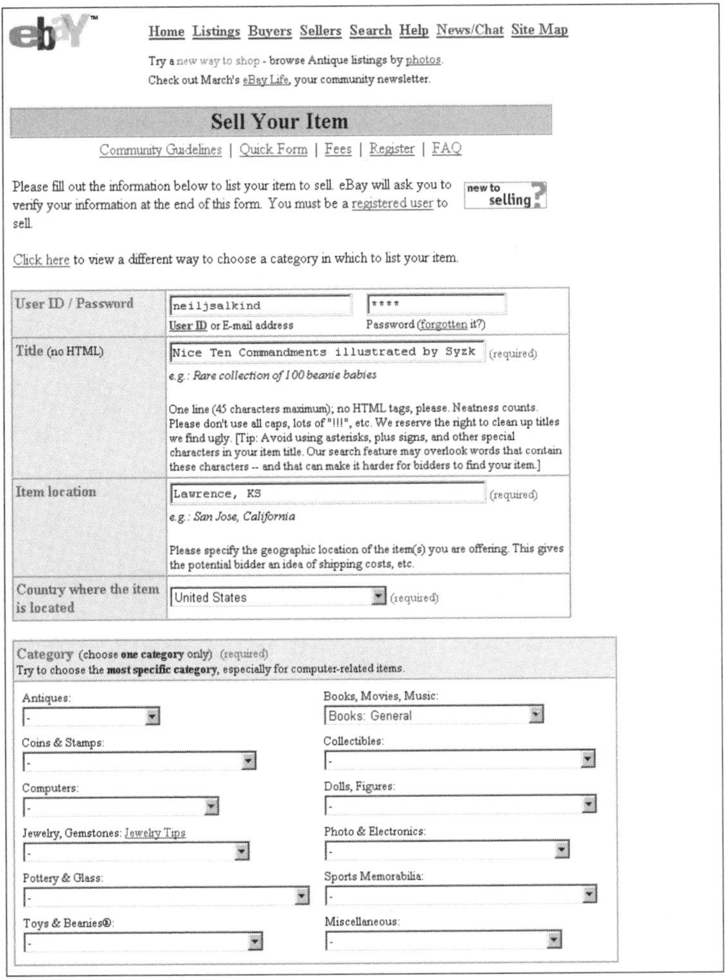

Figure 3.1 It looks like a lot of work, but listing an item to sell only takes a few minutes and is the first step towards being an eBay seller. *(continued on next page)*

Accepted Payment Methods (choose as many as apply)	☑ Money Order/Cashiers Check ☑ Personal Check ☐ Visa/MasterCard ☐ COD (collect on delivery) ☐ On-line Escrow ☐ American Express ☐ See Item Description ☐ Other ☐ Discover
Payment Terms	☐ Seller Pays ☐ Buyer Pays Fixed Amount ☐ Buyer Pays Actual Shipping Cost ☑ See Item Description
Shipping Terms	⦿ Ship to Home Country Only ○ Will Ship Internationally This information will indicate to users that they can bid on your item even if they live outside of your home country. Please note that most international buyers expect to send $US Dollars.
Description (HTML ok)	The Ten Commandments illustreated by Arthur Szyk. First 1993. Slight rubbing, and bumped corners. Szyk continues to draw attention for his phenomenally de during WWII in creating wokrs of patriotic art. This is to get started. (required) You may use HTML tags. Please, keep it neat! You'll have a chance to review how it looks before submitting your listing. Feel free to include links to your own graphics. Also, it is recommended that you include information about **who should pay for shipping**; this is a very common question. Also, don't use **quotes** in your HTML, since this will break your code. You can enter your primary image in the Picture URL section below. However, if you would like to add additional images to your description text here, you should include your image in the following HTML format: <img src=http://www.anywhere.com/mypicture.jpg > (Of course, you should replace http://www.anywhere.com/mypicture.jpg with your image URL, and include the < and > characters).
Picture URL	http:// (optional) If you have a URL to a picture, you may enter the URL here. By entering it here, the **PIC** icon will appear next to your item in the listings. Please click here if you want to view the eBay photo tutorial.
Quantity	1 (type numerals only) (optional) For Dutch auctions, enter the number of identical items you are offering for sale at this price. Otherwise, leave it as 1. Remember, if you are selling three items as one set to one buyer, then your quantity should be one, not three. **Multiple listings for identical items are not permitted, so you must use this option if you are selling multiple identical items**. Please enter only numerals in this field. Omit commas (','). Note: Read about the new requirements for Dutch Auctions.
Minimum bid	20 per item (numerals and decimal point '.' only) (required) e.g.: 2.00 This is the price at which the auction will start, and is, generally, the lowest price at which you are willing to sell your item. Setting this too high may discourage bidding! Omit currency symbols, such as dollar signs ('$') and commas (',')
Duration	7 ▾ days (required)
Reserve price	25 (numerals and decimal point '.' only) (optional) e.g.: 5.00 If you want to start the bidding at a price lower than you are willing to sell your item, use the Reserve Price option. This option is not popular among bidders! To use the Reserve Price option, set the real amount you are willing to accept for your item. This price will be hidden from bidders, but your item information will indicate whether or not the Reserve Price has been met. **Leave this blank** if you don't want a Reserve Price! Please refer to the Reserve Prices section of the Guidelines for more information. Note: Reserve Price items are not eligible for the Hot Items section. Also, Reserve Prices are not allowed for Dutch auctions.

Figure 3.1 It looks like a lot of work, but listing an item to sell only takes a few minutes and is the first step towards being an eBay seller. *(continued on next page)*

Boldface title?	☐ ($2.00 charge) (optional) For an additional fee of $2.00, you may choose to have your listing title appear in boldface in the listing pages, making it stand out among the other listings.
Featured Auction?	☐ ($99.95 charge) (optional) For a fee of **$99.95**, a Featured Auction listing will appear at the top of the main listings page, accessible from the top of every page on eBay. In addition, Featured Auctions are randomly selected for display on the main Home page and on category Home pages, though eBay does not guarantee that a specific auction will appear on either a category Home page or on the main Home page. You must have a feedback rating of at least 10 to place a Featured Auction.
Featured in Category?	☐ ($14.95 charge) (optional) For a fee of **$14.95**, a Category Featured Auction listing will appear at the top of the category listings page. In addition, Category Featured Auctions are randomly selected for display on category Home pages, though eBay does not guarantee that a specific auction will appear there. You must have a feedback rating of at least 10 to place a Category Featured Auction.
Great Gift icon? NEW!	☐ ($1.00 charge) (optional) For an additional fee of $1.00, you may choose to have a special 🎁 icon appear next to your listing title in the listing pages. This indicates that your item makes a great gift. The icon highlights your listing, and your item will appear in our special gift section. **Gift seller tip:** Indicate in your item description what special gift giving accomodations, if any, you will make. Please refer to Gift Icon for more information.
Private auction?	☐ Please don't use this unless you have a specific reason. (optional) This option specifies that bidders' identities not be visible on your auction page. Only the seller and the high bidder will be notified of the final outcome of the auction, and all bidders' addresses will be protected. For more information, see the Private auctions description. Not applicable for Dutch auctions. Most auctions are **not** private auctions. **Don't use this option** unless you have a specific reason; for example, avoiding embarrassment for buyers.

The Gallery NEW!

Gallery?	◉ Do not include my item in the Gallery ○ Add my item to the Gallery ($0.25 charge) ○ Feature my item in the Gallery (Featured fee of $19.95) (optional) The Gallery is currently available in the Antiques category. The Gallery will become available in other categories in the coming weeks.
Gallery Image URL	[http://] (optional) If you do not supply a URL for your Gallery image, your Pic URL will appear in the Gallery. (If you enter a picture URL in this field, you may use jpg, bmp, or tif files. Please note that **gif** files will **not** appear in the Gallery!)

You will be advised of all **fees** due before you place your listing. Press the "review" button below to see what fees are due immediately and what fees may be due if your item sells. You will not incur any fees until you accept the terms disclosed in the next screen.

Press [review] to proceed to the verification step.

Press [clear form] to start over.

Figure 3.1 It looks like a lot of work, but listing an item to sell only takes a few minutes and is the first step towards being an eBay seller.

3. Enter a title for the item; ensure that the title is no longer than 45 characters. This is the one line that appears on the

auction page that the buyer will first see, so follow these
suggestions to help increase the likelihood that it will sell:

—Make your item title short and to the point.

—Don't use any additional punctuation or characters (*, !, -,
and # for example).

—Spelling and grammar count, so be attentive to these
details.

Even more to the point, this one-liner is likely to decrease the
chances of a potential buyer finding what you are selling.

This is also why it's important to include key words that
increase the chances that an interested bidder will find your
item in a search. Include the type of item (the searcher may not
be in the category you have chosen), any names that identify it
(authors, characters, designers, manufacturers), and whatever
condition characteristics are used for the type of item you are
selling (very good, VG; first edition, 1st or 1ed.; mint in box, MIB;
or new in wrapper, NIW).

4. Enter the item location, which provides the bidder with
information about shipping costs (and for Big Ticket Items,
such as cars or boats, how far the buyer would have to
travel). You can enter a state, or a city, or a region.

5. Enter the country in which the item is being sold. The
default is the United States.

That's the first set of information you'll need. Now, let's move
into a more detailed description of the item and other important
seller details:

6. From the various drop-down menus you see in Figure 3.1,
select the one category that most specifically describes what
the item is.

7. Click on as many payment methods as you want to use.

To Charge or Not to Charge

Millions of merchants on and off the Internet allow for purchase using credit cards. Should you? If you want to accept payment using a credit card, you first have to make arrangements with your bank by opening an account. The benefits? Many buyers are used to the convenience of charging their purchases so it may increase the likelihood of a sale. In addition, as the seller, you know that a charged purchase represents good cash; the bank would not otherwise approve it. On the downside, there are significant costs associated with establishing and maintaining a credit card option. Remember also that the sponsoring bank takes a fee from the credit card transaction of anywhere from 1% to 5%, reducing any profit you might make. The buyer who uses a credit card has an easier time challenging payment if he or she is not satisfied. Because you will make every effort to satisfy your customer, this will not be a problem. If you're a once-in-a-while eBay seller, just take checks or money orders. If you intend to do lots of selling on eBay, seriously consider the card option.

8. Indicate the shipping terms. As you can see in Figure 3.1, the See Item Description option is the default. This is probably best since it provides the most flexibility. It's where you describe the payment terms in the description of the item.

9. Indicate if the item will be shipped only in the seller's home country or internationally.

10. Enter a description of your item with as much detail as necessary to inform the buyer exactly what you are offering, exactly what condition it's in (if relevant), and exactly what the payment and shipping terms are. The more exact you are on all these facets of your item, the less likely there will

be any misunderstanding between you and the bidder. It is actually easier to get bids on a low-quality item (like a beat-up copy of the first issue of *Sports Illustrated*) if you describe the wear and tear in detail. It gives the potential buyer a feeling of trust.

11. Enter the URL for any graphics that you might want to add to your description. (More about this later.)

12. Enter the number of lots you have to sell. A **lot** can contain more than one item—such as 22 volumes of the *Encyclopedia Britannica* that is sold as a single item. Unless this is a Dutch auction, the number is likely to be one.

13. Enter the minimum bid. This amount should always be the minimum amount of money that you are willing to sell the item for. You can set it wherever you want, but remember that the higher you set it (beyond what's reasonable for the item), the less likely it is that you will get bids. More people tend to bid when they see a low opening price. Some sellers set high bids to prompt you to email or call them and ask if the price is a mistake. They then sell you the item off eBay for a nice price and don't have to pay the fees. How can you tell? See if they have a lot of auctions with what you think are unreasonably high prices.

14. Indicate whether you want the auction to go for three, five, or seven days. It does not cost you any more to have a longer auction; it's just a matter of how long you want to attend to the auction and how fast you think the item will sell. You can always extend your auction.

15. Enter the **reserve price** (See **Question 53**) if you have one. This is the minimum price at which you are willing to sell an item. Keep in mind that reserve auctions are not a great deal of fun for the bidder since he or she never knows exactly where a bid stands. You could bid and bid and never get close to what the seller wants, which is frustrating.

16. Click the box in the Boldface Title? area if you want the title to appear in bold. If you think that such attention will help sell your item and it's worth the extra two dollars charge, do it. To the extent that what you are selling is essentially the same as dozens of other listings, this might be a worthwhile option. If you sell many items on eBay, why not spend the two bucks once as an experiment and see what happens?

17. If you want the item to be listed as a featured auction, click the box and get ready to pay the $99.95 fee to list it as such. You can read more about such actions in **Question 67**.

18. If you want the item to be featured in a category, click the box and get ready to pay the $14.95 fee to list it as such.

    For $1.00, you can attach the Great Gift icon to the item in the listing pages. If you do this, be sure to mention it in your description and describe what kinds of accommodations you are willing to make. For example, will you send it directly to the gift recipient? Will you gift wrap it? You can charge extra for these services just as long as you make it clear under the description.

20. Click on the Private Auction box if you want this auction to be private. See **Question 62** for more information about private auctions.

21. You can include your item in the Gallery for an extra 25 cents or have it featured for $19.95. You can also attach a graphic to the Gallery appearance by inserting the correct URL.

22. Click the button labeled Review and you're done!

Section 3   Selling

Verifying the Information

You will see a summary of all the information that was entered when you click the Review button (**Figure 3.2**). This shows the information eBay recorded for each of the steps listed, including any graphics that you might have added. Now's the time for you to look very carefully at what was entered and decide whether you want to keep the information as stated or use your browser's Back button and make any changes. Sometimes, this attempt to make a correction in the information that you just provided can fail. It's when you go back and the information you just entered is gone! Don't panic—just press the forward button on your browser and submit the listing. Then, click on the link with the address of the auction and click the revise link.

Home Listings Buyers Sellers Search Help News/Chat Site Map

Try a new way to shop - browse Antique listings by photos.

Check out March's eBay Life, your community newsletter.

Current account balance before adding this item: **0.00**.

Please verify your entry as it appears below. If there are any errors, please use the back button on your browser to go back and correct your entry. Once you are satisfied with the entry, please press the submit button.

Your User ID:	**neiljsalkind**
The title of the item:	**Nice Ten Commandments illustrated by Szyk**
Optional boldface title:	**no**
Featured auction:	**no**
Featured category auction:	**no**
Great Gift auction:	**no**
Optional Gallery:	**no**
Optional Featured Gallery:	**no**
The category of the item:	**Books, Movies, Music:Books:General**
Optional reserve price:	**$20.00**
Optional private auction:	**no**
Bidding starts at:	**$5.00**
Quantity being offered:	**1**
Auction duration in days:	**7 days**
Location of item:	**Lawrence, KS**
Country of item located:	**United States**
Money order/Cashiers checks:	**yes**
Personal checks:	**yes**
Visa/MasterCard:	**no**
Discover:	**no**
American Express:	**no**
Other:	**no**
OnlineEscrow:	**no**
COD (collect on delivery):	**no**
See Item Description for payment methods:	**yes**
Seller pays for shipping:	**no**
Buyer pays fixed amount for shipping:	**no**
Buyer pays actual shipping cost:	**no**
See item description for shipping costs:	**yes**
Will Ship Internationally:	**no**
The description of the item:	

The Ten Commandments illustrated by Arthur Szyk. First edition published by Gramercy Books, 1993. Very slight rubbing and bumped corners. Szyk continues to draw attention for his phenomenally detailed and colorful illustrations and for his role in WWII in creating works of patriotic art. This is a great way to get started collecting Szyk.

Picture URL

You have provided a URL to a picture of the item, which is shown below. If it shows up as a 'broken image', the URL may be incorrect, and you should go back and correct it. This can also occur if the image hasn't been loaded yet.

Picture URL: http://www.sunflower.com/~njs/images/10C.jpg

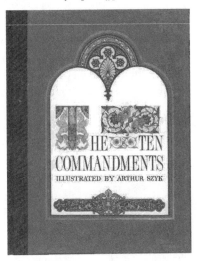

If this information is correct, please press the submit button to start the auction. Otherwise, please go back and correct it.

Fees:

- A non-refundable insertion fee of **$0.50** will apply to this listing immediately. This fee is due even if your item does not sell.

   Total Fees: $0.50

If your item receives bids, you will be charged a final value fee based on the closing value of the auction. This fee is 5.0% of the value up to $25, 2.5% of the value from $25 up to $1,000, and 1.25% of the value above $1,000. Complete information is in the Fees and Credits page.

Click this button to submit your listing. Click here to cancel.

submit my listing

Figure 3.2 Here's all the information that was entered, along with a nice graphic. Your listing is now ready to go up on eBay as an item that's ready to sell.

Once you are satisfied that the information you entered is correct, it's time to tell eBay to start the auction; click the Submit My Listing button.

Section 3   Selling

Viewing the Confirmation

Once you submit the item to be listed, eBay tells you that the auction has begun and indicates the item number you can use in your eBay activities. You also get an email message to that effect. As you can see in **Figure 3.3**, you also see a URL that takes you directly to that item. eBay gets lots of items from lots of people to place online each day, so you should not expect to see your item listed for at least one hour and it may even take longer. If your item does not appear, after eBay confirmed it, then email eBay at the help address we showed you earlier.

 Home Listings Buyers Sellers Search Help News/Chat Site Map

Try a new way to shop - browse Antique listings by photos.

Check out March's eBay Life, your community newsletter.

Auction has begun!

Your new ad has been saved. **IMPORTANT: your ad will not show up right away!** Listings are updated throughout the day, so your ad will be added at the next update.

Title of item: **Nice Ten Commandments illustrated by Szyk**
Your item number is: **73979187**

Keep these numbers! You will use this information, along with the e-mail address you entered, to identify yourself as the owner of this item. A confirmation message has been sent to you with the same information.

You may also use the following URL to refer to your auction item directly:

http://cgi.ebay.com/aw-cgi/eBayISAPI.dll?ViewItem&item=73979187

To increase traffic to your listing, you can post to appropriate newsgroups, listing the above URL. Please post only to appropriate newsgroups.

After adding this item, your account balance is now: **$-0.50**

You can edit your item as long as no one has left a bid. Choose the "Update Item" option on the View Item page for this item.

If you find you need to end your auction prior to the closing time, you may do so by using the **End auction** option from the **Seller Services Menu.**

Figure 3.3 Congratulations! Your item is now listed!

 ### How can I decide what kind of auction I should sponsor?

Which kind of auction is for you? **Table 3.1** shows a quick summary of the four types of auctions and when to use them.

Table 3.1—The Four Types of Auctions

Type of Auction	When to Use It	Advantages	Disadvantages
Regular	When you have an item to sell and are confident that it will draw a certain bid; it's priced so inexpensively that the price doesn't really matter.	Lets the market set the price for an item without interference. Because the price is left free to vary given the demand for the item, the bids could be way beyond expectation.	No guarantee that you will get the price you would have expected. Because the price is left free to vary given the demand for the item, the bids could be way below expectation.
Reserve	When you have an item to sell and want to make sure the winning bid is greater than a specific reserved price that the seller sets. This kind of auction is appropriate when you want to make sure you sell an item for a specified amount or not at all.	If the items sells, you are guaranteed to get at least the price you want. If the auction ends and the item did not sell, both the seller and the buyer are not obligated to complete any transactions.	The item may not sell at all unless you reach the reserve. Some bidders avoid reserve auctions.
Dutch	When you have more than one copy of an item to sell, all at the same set price. For example, you might have 50 copies of the same cookbook, which you are willing to sell at $15.00 each.	You can sell many items all at once (but you cannot set a reserve price).	If your price is to high, you may not get any bids at all.
Private	When you have an item to sell that you want to keep private from the rest of the eBay community.	You can develop a particular relationship with certain bidders who are interested in a particular item.	The lack of eBay community participation severely limits the bidding process.

A No No

Here are two emails you might find interesting.
It's a fairly common occurrence:

"Dear Seller,

*I have neither the time or desire to play the
bidding game, so I am contacting a couple of
people who accept credit cards and offer
products I want. I am interested in purchasing
either Visio 5.0 Standard or Pro. I am fine with
the CD-ROM and no-manual version. Please
advise as to your straight-out (no bid) price for
these items.*

> *Thank you,*
> *Robert"*

"Sir:

*If you do not want to bid on items, you shouldn't
be on eBay! eBay is not a shopping mall, and
it is not fair to other people if I merely state a
price and sell the item directly to you. This
solicitation is a violation of the eBay rules as I
understand them. Please visit a service like
http://www.outpost.com if you don't want to bid
on items.*

> *Eric"*

What's happening here? A browsing eBayer does not want
to participate in an auction, so he contacted the seller
directly (via the seller's email address) and let him know that
he would purchase the item without any bidding for a set
price. What's wrong with this? Nothing, other than that it
violates the intent of the eBay system (as Eric's response
indicates). When this happens, it's best to be as restrained
and polite as Eric and tell the other party to hit the road.

Too busy to complete the full form? eBay has a nice alternative: the Sell Your Item Quick form. You can find it at **http://pages.eBay.com/aw/newitemquick.html**. It's just a bit shorter, but may be just the time-saver you need.

Another way to save time if you become a regular seller on eBay is to save certain phrases or entire descriptions that apply to the items you are selling. You can copy and paste from one ad to the next. For example, you might always include, at the end of each listing description, "All my comics have a two-week money back guarantee. Add $3.00 for postage in the U.S. Checks take two weeks to clear."

I forgot to include something in the Sell Your Item Quick form. Can I change what appears in the listing?

You can change any part of the listing as long as you do it before the first bid has been received. This is like a grace period. You realized right after you submitted the listing that you made a mistake and want to correct it. For example, you may have forgotten to include shipping information in the description. You can revise information about your item as many times as you'd like, but you cannot change the quantity of items, any information about pricing, location, and the duration of the auction. You can even add a picture.

Follow these steps to amend the information on the sell form before a bid has been made:

1. Click Revise (which is found under the Update Item area on the item description).

2. Enter the changes you want to make.

3. Click the Submit button. The changes you made appear in the listing.

You can continue changing information as long as no bids have been received.

 **My listed item has a bid increment. What is that and where do I specify what it should be?**

The **bid increment** is the minimum amount of money between bids that eBay allows. eBay determines what this increment should be; that's why you didn't set it in the Sell Your Item Quick form. eBay does this based on the current bid, and the more expensive the item lists for, the higher the increment. Table 3.2 shows a summary of increments and item costs.

Table 3.2—Bid Increments

If the Current Bid Is...	The Next Bid Must Be at Least This Much Higher...
$.01–.99	$.05
$1.00–4.99	$.25
$5.00–24.99	$.50
$25.00–99.99	$1.00
$100.00–249.99	$2.00
$250.00–499.00	$5.00
$500.00–999.99	$10.00
$1,000.000–2,499.00	$25.00
$2,500.00–4,999.00	$50.00
$5,000 and up	$100.00

If you start an item at $25.00, the next bid that will be accepted by eBay has to be $26.00 or greater. The seller has no control over the bid increment.

I like what I have in the description, but I want to list the item under a different category. How can I do that?

You know that you can add to a listing—either words or pictures (**Question 65**)—but you can also change the category in which an item is listed. For example, you may have listed a particular book under the General subcategory but have since learned that it belongs under the Rare category.

Follow these steps to change the listing of an item:

1. Click on the site map link on any eBay page.
2. Click Change Item Category (located under Item Management under Seller Services). When you do this, you'll see the form shown in Figure 3.4.

Home Listings Buyers Sellers Search Help News/Chat Site Map

Protect yourself from listing or buying illegal or infringing items.

Manage all your transactions in one place -- My eBay, the best kept secret on eBay.

Changing your item's category

Use this form to change the category under which your item is listed. Please try to pick the most specific category.

Note: Some users (particularly Mac users) have reported problems with this page. If you experience a problem with this page, please try these alternate pages.

Your User ID:

Your Password:

The item number:

```
Antiques:General
Antiques:Ancient World
Antiques:Books, Manuscripts
Antiques:Folk Art
Antiques:Metalware
Antiques:Musical Instruments
Antiques:Prints
Antiques:Science Instruments
Antiques:Textiles, Linens
Antiques:Antiques (post-1900)
Books, Movies, Music:Books:General
Books, Movies, Music:Books:Rare
Books, Movies, Music:Books:Fiction:General
Books, Movies, Music:Books:Fiction:Adventure
Books, Movies, Music:Books:Fiction:Mystery
```

New Category:

Press this button to change the category of your listing:

[change category]

Press this button to reset the form if you made a mistake:

[reset form]

Figure 3.4 Changing your item's category is easy and may increase the chances of your item selling.

Section 3 Selling

3. Enter your user ID.

4. Enter your password.

5. Enter the item number.

6. Select the new category in which you want to list the item.

7. Click the button labeled Change Category.

From then on, the item will be listed in a new category. When an item does not sell, it's often because it is not in the correct category. Someone looking for a particular book, rather than using the search tools, goes to the category and only looks there.

If you are an active seller, it's a good idea to peruse the various categories that you are interested in. Not only will it give you an idea as to what types of items are listed for auction, but also of the prices that you can expect from a sale and where you should start the bidding.

 Have any great tips for selling?

Here's another set of top 10 tips:

1. Be as descriptive as possible when you list your item(s). Potential bidders always ask the question you least expect, so the more information you provide, the faster they can start bidding and the more sure everyone is that the sale will be a successful one. (They know exactly what you're selling and what condition it's in.) See **Question 83** for more about adding photos to the description.

2. Photos and descriptions sell auctions! A scanner or digital camera may be your best investment; visit a local Kinko's and save the scanned files to a disk. Be sure to save the file in JPG format. Try to make them less than 75K in size, but if you have to, larger is acceptable. People are much more comfortable buying items they can see.

3. Use the right type of auction. Remember that you can sell multiples of the same item in a Dutch auction, but most of the time you should use a regular auction with no reserve price. Private auctions should be used sparingly, if at all.

4. Check feedback. It's not only the bidder that has to be sure the seller is reputable, but the seller has to be sure that the bidder pays on time and stays in touch. Check and double check. If you have doubts, you can refuse to sell a particular item and explain your reasons. Other people want the item you listed as well.

5. Before you send out notices to winning bidders, check their feedback. Set strong but reasonable deadlines for responses and payment. If they miss these deadlines, warn them, but don't be afraid to re-list if you feel the person isn't going to pay. Just be sure to set the rules up front.

6. From the "more feedback is good" department: Check for other items a bidder has bid on, especially if you have some concern about being **deadheaded** (a bidder who does not pay). Often, you'll see that the bidder has also bid on the same item from other sellers. Odds are they will only pay for the one they get at the lowest price.

7. When you bid on an auction or list an item, be aware of when the auction(s) end and check for notices. Don't let too much time lapse. You should be responsible by following and closing transactions in a timely manner.

8. Be careful of checks drawn on foreign banks—and yes, Virginia, Canada is a foreign country. Your bank may charge fees for processing these checks. Ask either for a check drawn on a U.S. bank in U.S. dollars or a postal money order.

9. Remember that many bidders are not in your time zone! Think of your potential buyers and try to accommodate them. We've heard many complaints from people out of sync with U.S. time that they lose out on great items because the auctions end in the middle of their night.

10. Pack your items well. Use Tyvek liner envelopes or other water-resistant packing. Shipments are often ruined by water. Use lots of padding or stiffeners where needed. The key for flat items is often cardboard and more cardboard! Remember: Most people would rather pay a few cents more and get an item in great shape.

To Feature or Not to Feature

 I'm not sure whether to list my item as part of a featured auction. What do you think?

A **featured auction** finds an item at the top of the main Listings page, accessible from the home page and many other eBay pages. It is a place that a majority of eBayers visit on a regular basis. This high visibility should make the item easier to sell, but a featured auction costs almost $100.00 so the first consideration is the financial sense. After all, you will have to get back at least that, plus the cost of the item, to make it worth your while. A large number of listings in a featured auction are Dutch auctions, since many desirable items can be sold at once.

To make the featured auction an even sweeter deal, featured items are selected at random to appear on the featured display on the home page—right in the middle of the page. There's no guarantee that your item will appear there, but there's a good possibility since the listing changes each day.

There's no way to tell if the featured auction option works: Do more items sell this way than they would otherwise? The seller has to take his or her chances and see if the return is worth the investment.

Not only do you have to come up with the extra $100.00 to have an item included in a featured auction, but you must also have a feedback rating of at least 10, which means 10 more positives than negatives.

 There's another kind of auction: A category featured auction. How does that work and how is it different from a featured auction?

A **category featured auction** show the listing appearing at the top of the page for that category (such as the category featured item you see in **Figure** 3.5). Whereas a featured auction costs $99.95 to list, a category featured auction costs $14.95. Your category featured auction may appear on the home page associated with that category; they are also selected at random. (In Figure 3.5 that home page is Jewelry, Gemstones.) Like a featured auction, you need a feedback total of 10 to use this eBay option.

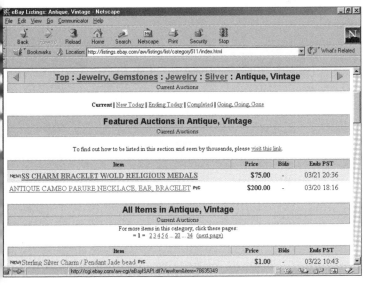

Figure 3.5 An example of a category featured item

 **Can I have any item featured?**

No. eBay has some very strict rules about what can and cannot appear in a featured auction. The no-nos include listings that:

▶ violate eBay guidelines

▶ are adult or sexual in nature

▶ are illegal or immoral

▶ are advertisements

▶ list firearms

▶ sell **auction utility software**. (This is the software that helps you bid and sell. See "Need Help?" at the end of this book for a description that can help you in your eBay activities.)

 **What happens if I later decide that I want to make the item I am selling a featured one?**

You're out of luck. It's too late to feature an already listed item. If you really want to do this, you have to cancel all the bids that have been received and start over.

The Money Part

 What do I pay eBay for conducting my auction?

It's surprisingly cheap. First, you have to pay eBay a small fee to have the item listed. That fee is charged immediately, so you will end with a negative balance no matter what. The fee is based on this table (**Table 3.3**) and will never be higher than $2.00. The total fee comes out to be about 6%. What a bargain! "Real" auction fees are usually 15%.

Table 3.3—eBay Listing Fee

Opening Minimum Bid or Reserve Price	Insertion Fee
$0.01–$9.99	$.25
$10.00–$24.99	$.50
$25.00–$49.99	$1.00
$50.00 and up	$2.00

The final fee that eBay collects (called the **final value fee**) is based on the final price for which the item sells (**Table 3.4**).

Table 3.4—eBay Final Value Fee

If an Item Sells for	eBay Takes This Percent of the Final Price (cumulative)
$.01–$25.00	5%
$25.01–$1,000.00	2.5% (plus above line)
$1,000.01 and up	1.25% (plus above two lines)

Both you (and eBay) benefit when the item sells for as much as possible. For example, a Pez dispenser (which sells for an opening minimum bid of $50.00) will bring $1.88 to eBay, plus the $2.00 fee to list the item. The entire transaction brings the eBay total to $3.88. You would come away with a little under $47.00.

eBay Fee Computation

There are lots of smart people on eBay. One of them is Eric Slone, who created a simple formula for computing the final value fee for an auction. You need to have Excel (or another spreadsheet program) and this simple formula:

```
=IF(PRICE<=25,PRICE*0.05,IF(PRICE<=1000,((PRICE-
  25)*0.025)+1.25,((PRICE-1025)*0.0125)+25.625))
```

Type the formula in a spreadsheet and replace PRICE
with a reference to the cell containing the final
auction price you want to calculate the fee for.
Here's what it all means:

Formula	What It Means
=IF(PRICE<=25,PRICE*0.05,	The fee is 5% if the price is <= 25.
IF(PRICE<=1000,((PRICE-25)*0.025)+1.25,	If the price is over $25.00, calculate a 2.5% fee on the amount over $25.00 and add a fee of 5% on the first $25.00.
((PRICE-1025)*0.0125)+25.625))	If the price is over $1,000.00, calculate a 1.25% fee on the amount over $1,000.00, add a fee of 5% on the first $25.00, and a fee of 2.5% on $975.00.

 **If I owe money, how do I get it to eBay?**

You start getting charged as soon as you start
listing items on eBay. At first it's just the listing fee; if you sell,
eBay collects its commission. As long as your account stays
under $10.00 (which won't be for very long), you won't have to
pay eBay; as soon as you owe more than that, the bill comes
due. Here are the payment options:

▶ You can send eBay a check or money order.

▶ You can have eBay automatically charge fees to your
credit card.

Here's a bit more about each of these options.

If You Want to Pay by Check

If you want to pay by check, follow these steps.

1. Go to the site map. Click Payment Coupon (which is found under Seller Services and Billing Information) and then provide the requested information. You'll see the payment coupon shown in **Figure 3.6**.

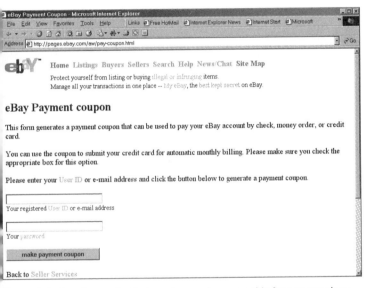

Figure 3.6 eBay charges for their services and you use this form to pay them.

2. Enter your user ID or email address.

3. Enter your password.

4. Click the button labeled Make Payment Coupon.

5. Print out the next page you see.

The payment coupon contains all the information that you need to send a payment to eBay, including addresses. Be sure that you read and understand the material that is located at the bottom of the payment coupon. For example, if you are paying through a foreign bank, a $10.00 U.S. dollars fee is charged. If you don't pay your balance, you are assessed a 1.5% monthly finance fee (which is 18% per year—a lot of extra money). Pay promptly.

If You Want to Pay by Credit Card

If you want to register or update a credit card, follow these steps:

1. Go to the site map and click Place or Update Your Credit Card Under Billing Information (which is found under Seller Services).

2. Enter your user ID or email address.

3. Enter your password.

4. Enter your name exactly as it appears on the credit card.

5. Enter the billing address for the credit card (which is probably your home or business address; it may not be if a company is to receive the bill).

6. Enter the credit card number using the following format: *xxxx-xxxx-xxxx-xxxx*. Here's where typing really counts. Don't forget the dashes and double check to be sure that the number is correct. You may accept American Express but eBay only accepts Visa and MasterCard.

7. Click the Submit button. Your credit card is billed for the expenses you incur.

You credit card application will be approved very quickly and you can check this by examining your account balance (**Question 73**).

Should I Charge My eBay Expenses?

There are advantages to charging. Primarily, you don't have to bother making any mail payments and there's no extra fee. The only disadvantage is the security of your charge card once it's in eBay's hands. In general, eBay makes every possible effort to make sure that such transactions and account

numbers are kept secure. They have a fancy-
schmancy secure server that keeps credit card
numbers inaccessible from everyone except the
system administrator. Since the majority of eBayers
do settle their account via credit card, it would be
senseless for eBay not to take these precautions.
eBay adds another incentive for registering a card
with them: When you do, they give you a $10.00
credit. What a deal! Our advice? Give them the card
and have fun.

**Now that I'm an eBay seller and I have an
account (which started as a result of my
first auction listing), how do I check my
eBay account balance?**

Follow these steps to check your eBay account status:

1. Go to the site map and click the Place or Update Your Credit
   Card (which is located under Seller Services).

2. Enter your user ID or email address.

3. Enter your password.

4. Enter the amount of activity you want to see (for example,
   since the last invoice, the last day, the last week, or
   something similar).

5. Click the View Account button.

As you see in **Figure 3.7**, Account Status lists your

▶ Account name

▶ Account ID

▶ Whether a credit card is on file

▶ The last four digits of your credit card number

▶ Credit card expiration date and the most recent date that
   credit card information was updated

Finally, toward the bottom of the form, you'll find detailed transaction information including your eBay balance.

Account Status for neiljsalkind (E1151327)

Account Balance: **9.50**

Account Name	neiljsalkind
Account Id	E1151327
Credit Card on file:	Yes
Credit Card Info:	4313 Exp: 09/01/00
Credit Card Update:	03/04/99 09:45

Ref #	Date	Type	Item	Credit	Debit	Balance
96403516	03/04/99 08:46	Insertion fee	73979187	-	-0.50	-0.50
96427488	03/04/99 09:43	Credit Card on file -- Thank You!		10.00	-	9.50
		CC New Authorization				
		Account Balance				9.50

Figure 3.7 Check your account status frequently to know exactly what your balance is.

How often should I check my account?

Good eBayers check their account status all the time. Know why? Because mistakes happen and when they do and you think that your account balance might be wrong, it's time to contact eBay directly and see if you can set things straight. Another good reason to check your account status is to see what you may owe eBay for their services.

Are there any circumstances where I can get eBay's commission refunded to me?

There are several circumstances when you can get a refund of the final value fee (never the listing fee). You have to make a request (which is discussed momentarily). You can receive a full credit if any of the following have occurred:

▶ You have attempted to contact the high bidder but have had no success.

▶ The high bidder didn't send payment.

▶ The high bidder's payment was not good (for example, the check bounced).

▶ The item was returned to you, the seller.

▶ For whatever legitimate reason (such as a medical emergency), the high bidder could not continue the transaction.

You can receive a partial credit when the following have occurred:

▶ The sale price was lower than the highest bid.

▶ The high bidder refused to complete the transaction, but you sold it to another bidder.

Q76 How do I apply for such as refund credit?

You need to complete a Final Value Fee Credit Request form. However, you have to wait three days after the auction has ended before completing the form. That gives you time to resolve some of the reasons you are asking for a credit in the first place. Follow these steps to complete a Final Value Fee Credit Request form:

1. Go to **http://pages.eBay.com/aw/credit-request.html**.
2. Provide your user ID.
3. Provide your password.
4. Provide the item number of which you want a complete or partial refund.
5. Click the Submit button.

Q77 I checked my account balance and have more than $35.00. Can I get this back?

Yes, but you should consider leaving it in—especially if you intend to continue your eBay activities. It's easier than having to write out a check to eBay every week.

Section 3 Selling

To request a refund, follow these steps:

1. Click the site map in any eBay Web page.

2. Click Account Refunds (which is located under Billing Information).

3. Print out the form you see in **Figure 3.8**.

4. Complete the form and send it to eBay (via U.S. mail) or fax it to eBay at the number on the form.

eb**Y**™   Home Listings Buyers Sellers Search Help News/Chat Site Map

Protect yourself from listing or buying illegal or infringing items.
Manage all your transactions in one place -- My eBay, the best kept secret on eBay.

eBay Account Refund Request

* eBay will gladly issue you a refund for a credit balance on your eBay account over $1.00.
* All refund requests must be in writing.
* Print, complete, and sign this form. Mailing and faxing information is below.
* To request a credit for a completed auction, click here.

Email address of seller: _____

Name of seller: _____

Address of seller: _____

_____

Please refund me $ _____ from my eBay account.

Any additional information? _____

Your signature and date: _____

Mail or fax this form to eBay at:

eBay Inc. - Billing Department - Refund Request
2005 Hamilton Ave., Suite 350
San Jose, CA 95125 USA
FAX: 1-408-558-7404 (no cover page, please)

Back to Seller Services

Figure 3.8 To get any kind of a refund you have to print out this form, complete and mail it to the friendly eBay accountants.

Canceling an Auction

**Q78** **Are there any circumstances under which I can cancel an auction once it's started? Is that unfair to the bidders?**

You can cancel an auction (or **end it early**, as eBay refers to this action). It can be unfair, but you may need to do it for a variety of reasons. Perhaps, for example, you have to leave town and will not be able to monitor the auction's progress. You may have changed your mind about selling the item at all.

The biggest downside of ending an auction early is that many eBayers wait until the last minute to sneak in their bid and you may lose a really high bidder. Consider that when you make your decision to end the auction earlier than scheduled.

To end an auction, follow these steps:

1. Click on the site map link on any eBay Web page.
2. Click on the End Auction Early link (which is located under Item Management).
3. Enter your user ID.
4. Enter your password.
5. Enter the item number.
6. The auction is ended when you click the End Auction button.

Even if you end your auction early, you are still responsible for honoring the high bid. If you ended the auction early because you no longer want to sell the item (your younger brother found out!), you need to cancel all the bids that have already been made.

 **My younger brother wants my father's old radio; but I put it up for auction. I have to stop the auction and cancel all the bids. How do I do it?**

We just showed you how to end an auction early. Follow these steps to cancel all the bids that have already been made.

1. Click on the site map link on any eBay page.

2. Click on the Cancel a Bid link (which is located under Item Management).

3. Enter your user ID.

4. Enter your password.

5. Enter the item number.

6. Enter the user ID of the bid you are canceling.

7. Explain, in fewer than 80 characters, why you are canceling this bid.

8. Click the Cancel Bid button.

Canceling one bid isn't any fun and canceling a bunch is really not fun. Don't forget: If you want to end an auction early and do not want to sell the item you listed, you have to go through these steps for every single bidder.

eBay and Web Site Stuff

 **I have a business Web site that is directly related to my eBay selling activities. Is there any way that I can link my Web site to eBay?**

There are two types of buttons (**Figure 3.9**) that you can have installed on your Web site. The first, when clicked on your home page, takes you to eBay's home page. The second, when clicked on your home page, goes to the sale items list. Both of these can bring attention to eBay (which eBay likes) and to the list of items that you are selling.

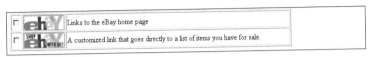

Figure 3.9 The two eBay buttons that you can link to your home page.

Placing these items on your home page takes some knowledge of HTML (Hypertext Markup Language), but with a little effort almost anyone can do it. HTML is the programming language that makes Web pages appear as they do on your screen. For example, each element you see on eBay's opening home page has HTML code that corresponds to that element.

This first set of steps simply tells eBay your intentions. It won't place the buttons on your home page. You have to do that by changing the HTML code that controls the way your home page appears. Follow these steps to place one or both of these buttons on your home page:

1. Click on the site map on any eBay Web page.

2. Click Link Buttons (which is located under General Seller Information).

3. Select the buttons you want to display on your home page. You can click

   ▶ Links to the eBay home page

   ▶ A customized link that goes directly to a list of items you have for sale or both

4. Enter your user ID.

5. Enter your password.

6. Enter the URL of the home page where you plan to display the buttons.

7. Read the legal shtick and then click the I Agree button.

Section 3 Selling

Once you have gone through these steps, eBay provides you with instructions for installing the buttons on your site. This consists of placing certain HTML commands in the source code for your home page. Here's the exact code that needs to be inserted for a link to eBay's home page:

```
<a href="http://pages.ebay.com/linkButtons">
<img src="http://pics.ebay.com/aw/pics/
ebay_gen_button.gif" alt="eBay Home"> </a>
```

Here's the exact code that needs to be inserted for a link to your seller list:

```
<a href="http://cgi3.ebay.com/aw-cgi/ebayISAPI.dll?
ViewListedItemsLinkButtons&userid=neiljsalkind">
<img src="http://pics.ebay.com/aw/pics/
ebay_my_button.gif" alt="My items on eBay"> </a>
```

Substitute your user ID for neiljsalkind in the second line.

In **Figure 3.10** you can see how the link to the eBay home page was added to another home page. Just a click on the eBay link takes you to the home page.

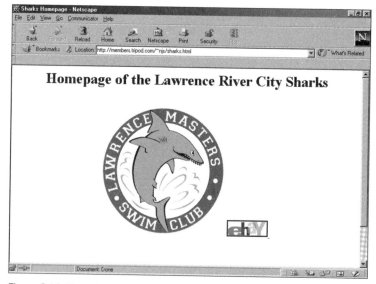

Figure 3.10 How about those Sharks? eBay is just a click away form the Sharks home page.

Can I use other HTML codes in my description?

You can paint the town (or your description) red with HTML codes to make things look cooler than the plain text that sellers often use. Take a look at the description in **Figure 3.11**.

Description

Rubaiyat of Omar Khayyam illustrated by famous artist Arthur SZYK! Translated by Edward Fitzgerald, The Heritage Press, New York, 1946. Beautiful decorated blue and cream covers designed by Szyk (pictured below). Eight lithographed color illustrations printed on double leaved pages. Each illustration is worthy of framing! Includes fair gold metalic slipcase. Well protected, very nice copy! There is NO reserve on this book and a must for any Szyk fan. See my other Szyk auctions and combine shipping costs.

Buyer pays actual shipping costs by U.S. Mail or Federal Express; I will ship internationally for actual, added costs. You can pay for your auctions by check (please be patient as I will wait for your check to clear), money order, or credit card. You can pay via my credit card server. I can accept the following credit cards:

Orders paid by credit card ship immediately. Any questions? Please feel free to email me at eslone@scs-intl.com, visit my eBay homepage, or my company homepage. If you have any special concerns, please ask before bidding!

Check out our HOT software for eBay: The Watcher. The Watcher will monitor your auctions and advise you on the current bid status and also when you get new bids on items - all in an easy to use Windows program. Visit our website today and download a FREE demo copy and see how powerful this program is! The Feedback Wizard. Allow you to enter all of your feedback in one easy form, then send it to eBay in a single batch. No more waiting for slow-loading forms!

Figure 3.11 An elaborate description created using HTML codes. And, it's easier than you think to do!

What's special about this description and how was it done?

You can't see it in the figure, but the print appears in different colors. Here's the HTML code that makes all the text that follows appear in green on a computer monitor:

```
<font color="#008000"> is the HTML code for green
```

There is an Internet link (**http://www.scsintl.com/ creditcard.htm**) to the seller's credit card server. This means that the high bidder can click on this link and pay by credit card through a secure transaction. Here's how he entered the code so that a click on the link takes you to the secure card server:

```
You can pay via my credit card server at
   <a href="http:
//www.scs-intl.com/creditcard.htm">
http://www.scs-intl.com/creditcard.htm</a>.
```

The credit card logo in the middle of the description changes from Discover to MasterCard to Visa. How did he do it? Here are the HTML commands:

```
src="http://www.scs-intl.com/images/CreditCard.gif"
border="0" width="100" height="64" align=
"middle" alt="MasterCard - Visa -
   Discover"></font></p>
```

There are links to the seller's email address, his eBay home page. His company home page and special software he sells (The Watcher and The Feedback Wizard) are described in the "Help" section of Section 1, "Getting Started."

```
Orders paid by credit card ship immediately.
Any questions? Please feel free to email me at
<ahref="mailto:eslone@scs-intl.com">
eslone@scs-intl.com</a>, visit my <a href=
"http://members.ebay.com/aboutme/eslone/">
eBay homepage</a>, or my <ahref="http://www.
scs-intl.com">company homepage</a>.
If you have any special concerns,
please ask before bidding!</font></big></p>
```

There's a cool flashing form at the bottom of the page listing what else the seller has for sale as well as the seller's business logo:

```
<p align="center"><a href="http://www.scs-intl.com">
<img src="http://www.scs-intl.com/images/SCSAd.gif"
 alt="Scientific Consulting Services" WIDTH="468"
HEIGHT="60" border="0"></a><font color="#000080">
   <br></p>
```

All of these elements are added in the item description. How easy are they to add? Very. All you need to do is follow the instructions listed earlier. How easy is it to know which HTML code to add? That's a little bit harder. Read on.

eBay and Business: #1

The owners of a supply company write:

"We utilize eBay's auctions because it is a very effective, low-cost method of selling...but an even better form of very inexpensive advertising! We use a link to our Web site. Along with an HTML Web page loaded onto their server, for the individual products we have for sale.

The Y2K situation brings a large, growing audience and eBay is used by more and more people looking for about anything. It is just a great form of advertising and sales for us and people enjoy it!

Where else can you go and buy "Big Mac's" record-breaking home run baseball ... or buy a water filter or a food package from us ... all in a few minute's time! People always spend hours on eBay versus browsing the Web where you may spend 2—3 minutes per site. Good luck!"

—*Steve from Oregon*

How can I find out which HTML codes control which elements on the screen and what they will look like?

The answer to this question is a whole other book in itself, but we can give you some simple commands to enhance the appearance of your items. You can find a complete listing of HTML codes and what they do including lots of examples at http://www.authors.com/htmlref.htm.

Table 3.5 has a few commands to get you started. The most important thing to remember about using HTML is that tags are placed at the beginning and ending of the material that you want affected, and special commands are used to create special elements such as tables.

Table 3.5—Basic HTML Starter Tags

Tag	Appears Like This in the Item Description
<font size>Great New Item!<font size=+6>	Great New Item!
<font size>Great New Item!<font size=+5>	Great New Item!
<font size>Great New Item!<font size=+4>	Great New Item!
<font size>Great New Item!<font size=+3>	Great New Item!
<font size>Great New Item!<font size=+2>	Great New Item!
<font size>Great New Item!<font size=+1>	Great New Item!
<B>This text appears in Boldface.</B>	**This text appears in bold face**
<I>eBay sure is fun.</I>	*eBay sure is fun*
<U> This text appears underlined.</U>	This text appears underlined
<c>This text will be centered on the page </c>	This text will be centered on the page
<ADDRESS>njs@sunflower.com</ADDRESS>	njs@sunflower.com
Tag	**Performs This Function**
 	Creates a break at the end of a line
<P> </P>	Creates a paragraph
<HR width=% of page>	Creates a horizontal lines

For example, here's a simple item description, and the accompanying code that was used to create it:

Finally, It's Here!

First time offered on eBay!
The coolest toys in the world.

This collection of Froibles is bound to please
anyone from 9
to 90 years old.

Questions? Contact the seller at
njs@sunflower.com

```
<center><font size=+2>Finally, It's Here!</font>
<br>First time offered on eBay!
The coolest toys in the world.
<br>This collection of Froibles is bound to please
<i>anyone</i> from 9
to 90 years old.
<br>
<hr WIDTH="100%">
<p><b>Questions? Contact the seller at </p>
<a href="/njs@sunflower.com">njs@sunflower.com</a>
</b></center>
```

Beware of Shill Bidders

Be careful of people who have more than two accounts on your auction; they may be setting up to manipulate the price. People who do this are called shill bidders. Here's a simple example of how this can work: By bidding using a false account, such a bidder can discover the lowest price you are willing to accept for an item. He or she bids at a very high price and then bids using another account and come up as the second highest bidder. When the bidder does not pay for the auction on the first account (much to the seller's frustration), it is unknowingly offered to the second highest bidder, which is the same person. Shill bidding can also be used by a seller to increase the bid amount. Shilling is wrong, illegal, and against eBay policy!

Adding Images to Your Auction

 How can I add an image to an item's description?

Some of the coolest eBay items contain pictures. Can I do that? "The more you tell, the more you sell" might as well be the eBay motto of the month. Any words, pictures, and information that you can provide increase the chances that your attempt at selling will be successful.

Remember the item for sale that you saw in Figure 3.2? Unless you knew something about the dramatic illustrations that Szyk has done before, you would really not understand the beauty of his work. Use a graphic, image, picture—whatever you can muster—whenever possible. Believe it or not, it's not very difficult to do.

The basic logic is to take an image of the item you want to sell and store it somewhere on the Word Wide Web. You then tell eBay where it's stored and the listing you want it to be shown in. There are three steps involved in getting an image of your item on to the eBay listing:

1. Create an electronic image of the item and edit it.

2. Transfer the image to a location on the Word Wide Web.

3. Change your item description so there is a reference to the electronic image. If you have yet to list the item, specify such on the selling form.

Create an Electronic Image

The first step is to create an electronic image of the item you want to sell. How you do this depends upon what you are selling.

If you are selling something that's two dimensions (such as a certificate, stamp, or a book cover that is 2 dimensional), you can simply scan the image using one of many different types of color scanners. Color scanners are now available for less than

$100.00 and if you ask around your neighborhood, look around your child's school or your own businesses, you'll probably find one that you can use. If you can't find a scanner to use, your local print shop, copy center (such as Kinko's), or public library probably has one. Expect to be charged for this service.

If you are selling an item that is three dimensions (such as perfume bottle), just about the only way to get an image in your description is to use a digital camera to take a photograph. Digital cameras are the new way of taking and storing pictures. No film. Rather, the picture is stored either in a storage device in the camera or on a special floppy disk that you can also place in your computer's disk drive. In either case, once the digital picture is taken, it then needs to be transferred to your computer and saved as a file in either .jpg or .gif format. This technology should not intimidate you; it's really simple.

Like scanners, digital cameras are pretty easy to find around school or work. You could borrow one to see whether taking such pictures would be a big help in making your item descriptions more attractive. Digital cameras cost between $350.00 and $1,000.00 and are lots of fun, although lacking in taking a picture with very high resolution (which regular cameras have always done quite well).

No Digital Camera? No Sweat!

Everywhere you look, there are businesses that support eBay activities. For example, there are several companies that will take your photograph, create an electronic file, and then transfer it to an Internet site of your choice. Using these companies, you skip the first two steps necessary for getting an image into your item description.

What companies? Try the following:

▶ PhotoNet (**http://www.photonet.com/**) allows you to take your film to one of their cooperating stores or send it in. When you bring it in, you check off the PhotoNet

Online option. When your film is developed, the images are also placed on the Internet. You can access the photos, work with them as you see fit, including sending them to friends and family or downloading them to the Internet site you will use in the item description.

▶ Seattle FilmWorks (**http://www.filmworks.com/**) offers similar service where your film is developed and images are available through the Photo Mail service. They too can be downloaded and shared. They're in electronic format, so anything you do with any electronic file can be done with these files as well.

Scan the image and save it as a .jpg file, which is what eBay prefers (although .gif will work).

Once the electronic file is created, you can use any one of many different types of software to edit it as needed. Most installations of Windows and the Macintosh come with simple software already installed (such as Paint or Imaging for Windows) and you can use them to crop, to change the coloring of, or to tweak the size of the image. There are bunches of killer software (available for hundreds of dollars) that you can purchase, such as Adobe Photoshop. These high-end programs can be used to edit, as well as to create special effects.

Finally, there's another option for capturing images to use on eBay—a USB or PCI-based camera which is less than $100.00. It works great for taking snapshots of the kind of stuff that can't be scanned.

Transfer the Image to the Word Wide Web

If there's any part of the process that is sometimes cumbersome, this is it.

The goal is to get the information from its location on your computer to an Internet site. eBay will then reference that site when it displays your item in an auction. The image should appear as well.

Using the space provided by your Internet provider gives you most control over what images go where. Most Internet providers—AT&T, AOL, Earthlink, and Mindscape, for example—provide space for each of its clients' home pages (whether you build one or not). You need to know two things in order to transfer an image:

1. The location of the file you want transferred on your computer.

2. How to connect to your Internet Service Provider so that you can place the image you captured in your Web space. Tell eBay to refer to that Web space when looking for a picture of an item.

Transfers of files usually take place via a special program. In other words, you have to send or upload it from your computer to your provider's computer, which has the space that you need. One of these programs is CuteFTP, a simple program that transfers files from your hard drive to the Internet site, where you can store files. You can get CuteFTP at **http://www.shareware.com**; download and install it on your computer.

If your Internet service provider doesn't provide space for you, you can use one of several services that helps eBay customers and will host your images for a small fee. How small? One company, WeppiHeke (**http://www.weppiheka.com/**) charges $.40 per month. Another, Images R Us (**http://www.imagesrus.net/**) charges $.20 per month and has available free backgrounds and artwork.

Here's a list of others you can contact to get some idea about charges and services. These services are becoming increasingly popular and some don't even have any more room for hosting pictures. You should get onboard as soon as possible if you're interested.

▶ ImageHost. The first image is free.
  http://www.imagehost.com/

▶ Service For You. Scans and edits as well as hosts.
  http://www.images4u.net/services.htm

▶ Show Your Stuff. Scans, edits, and hosts.
http://members.xoom.com/zina/showyourstuff

▶ SmartBirds. Provides hosting and scanning.
http://www.psnw.com/~smartbird/hosting.htm

▶ Zeldari. Open all night!
http://www.zeldas.com/Imaging.htm

▶ Picture This. Has a link to starting a new eBay auction.
http://www.javanet.com/~markr/

▶ ImageHosting. Charges $.25 per image.
http://www.imagehosting.com/general/hosting.html

▶ Final Frontier. Stores all your images for $10.00 per year and
a $5.00 setup fee. **http://www.finalfront.com/storage.htm**

▶ MrPics. Charges by the kilobyte rather than by the picture.
http://www.mrpics.com/

▶ The BestShots. Edits, crops, and resizes at no extra charge.
http://www.thebestshots.com/

Point to the Image Within eBay

Here's the last step. You have your image and it's available on
the Internet. Now you have to tell eBay where to find it. This is
the easiest part of all.

Every one of the electronic images you transferred to a storage
place on the Internet has a URL or a Web page address. For
example, in Figure 3.2, you can see an image of a book cover.
The URL for that image is **http://www.sunflower.com/
~njs/images/10c.jpg**.

That's the exact location of the image. To use it in an item
description, you have to enter it in the appropriate place in the
Sell Your Item from which you saw in Figure 3.1. This is part of
the long form that you completed (see **Question 61**) when you
started to list this item. Once your sell form is complete, the
image will appear in the description.

 Can I add an image to a description after an auction has started?

Yes. Follow these steps if you want to add an image to an item after the auction has started:

1. Using your browser, go to the following eBay Web page:
   http://pages.ebay.com/aw/add-to-item.html

2. Enter your user ID in the form you see in **Figure 3.12**.

---

ebY™   Home Listings Buyers Sellers Search Help News/Chat Site Map

Protect yourself from listing or buying illegal or infringing items.
Manage all your transactions in one place -- My eBay, the best kept secret on eBay.

Adding to your item description

Use this form to add more information to your item description. In order to prevent possible abuse, you cannot completely replace your item description. The information you add here will be appended to your current description.

Your User ID: [   ]
Your password: [   ]
The item number: [   ]

The text to add to your description:

[   ]
[   ]
[   ]   (HTML ok)

To add a picture to your item description, use the following HTML code:
<img src=http://www.anywhere.com/mypicture.jpg>

Simply replace http://www.anywhere/mypicture.jpg with the complete URL of a picture on your own web site. Be sure to include the < and > in the HTML code. The photo will appear in your item description.

For more information on including picture with your listing, excellent tutorials are available at:
http://www.pongo.com/tutorials/aweb-images and http://www.twaze.com/aolpix. These tutorials are maintained by members of eBay community, and eBay is not responsible for their content or accuracy.

Press this button to review and add this to your listing:

[review]

Press this button to clear the form if you made a mistake:

[clear form]

Figure 3.12 Adding information (including an image) to your item's description.

3. Enter your password.

4. Enter the number of the item.

5. Enter the additional text that you would like to add to the description.

6. Enter the following HTML code to add a picture or pictures to the item description:

```
<img src=http://www.anywhere.com/mypicture.jpg>
```

You need to replace the **www.anywhere.com/mypicture.jpg** with the location where the image is stored.

7. Click the Review button. eBay displays the complete description with the addition you are adding. Now's the time to review the addition and decide whether it appears as you would like. You can add at this point, but you cannot edit the existing description. If you want to begin all over, click Clear Form.

8. If the description is as you want, click Add to Description. The new description will appear on the Auction page. If you want to change what you are adding, use the Back button on your browser, change the material (including the image), and continue with step 7.

 **I did all that to get an image in the description, but it doesn't work. What did I do wrong?**

There are a few things that you can check:

▶ Make sure that you have entered the URL for the image correctly in the Sell form. Accurate typing really, really counts.

▶ Make sure that the URL is correct. You should be able to enter it in the Internet browser that you use and see the image.

▶ If you are using an image hosting service, be sure that it is online and working. Go to their Web site and see if you can retrieve the image that the service is hosting for you.

▶ Confirm that you saved the image as a .jpg when it was stored. Otherwise, eBay may not be able to see it.

Remember this, however, about having eBay point to an image: The image isn't stored on any of eBay's computers, nor does the storage of the image have anything to do with eBay.

After the Sale

 **What is the best way to notify the highest bidder that the auction is over and payment arrangements need to be made?**

As you probably realize by now, eBay keeps you informed throughout the auction what's happening and will notify you once the auction is done. Here's a sample letter from eBay notifying the seller that the auction has ended and what the final high bid was. The high bidder is notified as well.

Section 3 Selling

Dear neiljsalkind and jwidome,
DO NOT REPLY TO THIS MESSAGE. PLEASE ADDRESS YOUR
MAIL DIRECTLY TO BUYER OR SELLER.
****
Protect yourself from listing or buying illegal or
infringing items.
See http://pages.ebay.com/aw/help/topics-png-
items.html
****
BUYERS PLEASE REMIT PAYMENT TO SELLER
This message is to notify you that the following
auction has ended:
  Nice Ten Commandments illustrated by Szyk (Item
#73979187)
  Final price: 61.00
  Auction ended at: 03/11/99 08:46:20 PST
  Total number of bids: 9
  Seller User ID: neiljsalkind
  Seller E-mail: njs@sunflower.com
  High-bidder User ID: jwidome
  High-bidder E-mail: jwidome@erols.com
Seller and high bidder should now contact each other
to complete the sale. IMPORTANT: buyer and seller
should contact each other within three business days,
or risk losing their right to complete this
transaction. The official results of this auction
(including e-mail addresses of all bidders) can be
found for 30 days after the auction closes at:
http://cgi3.ebay.com/aw-cgi/eBayISAPI.dll?ViewItem&
item=73979187. If you won an auction in which the
seller has at least a positive feedback rating of 10,
you can send a gift alert. This is a great feature if
you're buying gifts or if you're a little late on
your gift-giving. To use this feature, see:
http://cgi3.ebay.com/aw-cgi/eBayISAPI.dll?ViewGift
Alert&item=73979187&userid=jwidome
If you have trouble contacting each other via email:
http://pages.ebay.com/aw/user-query.html
Please leave feedback about your transaction:
http://cgi2.ebay.com/aw-cgi/eBayISAPI.dll?
LeaveFeedbackShow&item=73979187 For other valuable
"after the auction"
needs: http://pages.ebay.com/aw/postauction.html
****

```
eBay has a new mailing address for sellers who mail
checks
and money orders:
eBay, Inc.
P.O. Box 200945
Dallas, TX 75320-0945
This address is for check and money order payments
only!
All other correspondence should still be mailed to:
eBay, Inc.
2005 Hamilton Avenue, Ste 350
San Jose, CA 95125
********************************************************
Thank you for using eBay! If you have not already
done so today, it wouldn't hurt to mention eBay to a
few of your friends!
http://www.ebay.com
_____

Item Description:
The Ten Commandments illustrated by Arthur Szyk.
First edition published by Gramercy Books, 1993. Very
slight rubbing and bumped corners. Szyk continues to
draw attention for his phenomenally detailed and
colorful illustrations and for his role in WWII in
creating works of patriotic art. This is a great way
to get started collecting Szyk.
On 03/04/99 at 08:51:10 PDT, seller added the
following information:
Buyer pays $3.00 postage.
```

As the seller, the first thing that you should do is notify the buyer that the auction has ended and that it's time to make payment arrangements. If you performed your seller job well, all terms have already been agreed upon (shipping, postage, and who handles what). This letter should be a matter of rephrasing those terms and letting the high bidder know what to do next.

Here's a wonderful sample letter that you might use to notify the highest bidder that the auction is over and that that person won. This is to Bill, who was the highest bidder on a Tiffany vase:

Dear Bill:

eBay has just notified me that you are the successful bidder on the Tiffany vase and it's time for us to confirm payment and shipping arrangements.! The item number is 73979187. Shipping for this item is $4.50 including insurance and if you have bid on other items I have listed for auction and would like the orders combined to save on postage, please let me know. Payment can be made by check, money order, or credit card (MasterCard, Visa, or Discover). If you are uncomfortable sending your credit card information over the Internet, you may fax it or call me at the numbers below. If you get my voice mail,please leave the information there. I am the only person who checks messages. Please note that credit card charges will show on your statement under my company name, B&H Enterprises.

VERY IMPORTANT — PLEASE READ:

You must respond that you have received this email and provide your mailing address in an email within 5 days and I need to receive payment within 14 days from the close of auction. Please include a note with the item number and name you have won with your payment. We do everything to assure that items are in good condition as described in the listing at the time of shipment. We try to pack each item carefully to protect it during shipment. However, problems occur and we will do whatever we can to help resolve the problem. All we ask is that you contact us and let us know your concerns. If you are not pleased with the item and would like a refund, we need you to contact us before you send it back. Please visit my homepage at www.b&H.com for more information about eBay auctions and other things we sell.

Thanks,

Lew

Q87 What if the high bidder doesn't contact me?

If you set some guidelines (such as five days to email a letter like the one previously shown), try contacting the bidder again by email or phone (if he or she provided you with that information).

Here's the next letter to Bill:

```
Dear Bill:
It has been a week since you were sent emails
about items you won from me on eBay. I really
need a response from you with your address so I
can plan to send you the item. You also need to
send me payment. I have not received anything to
date. I really don't want to re-list the item,
but will be forced to if I do not hear from you
in 3 days.
Thanks,
Lew
```

Q88 What if I can't find the bidder's email address or contact information? How do I get it?

You need to send out a registered user information request, which asks eBay to provide you with contact information for any registered user. To complete such a request, follow these steps:

1. Click the site map link on any eBay Web page.

2. Click Contact Other Registered User (which is located under Registered User Services).

3. Provide your user ID.

4. Provide your password.

5. Provide the user ID of the eBayer for whom you want contact information.

6. Click Send Request.

7. The information will arrive via email and you can use it to contact the other user. You can also use this same procedure to contact any eBayer who is registered.

Q89 What if the bidder responds to my email saying that he will be sending payment, but is late?

Here's the perfect letter for that situation:

```
Dear Bill:
It has been a week since you were sent emails
about items you won from me on Bay. You indicated
that you would be sending payment. I have not
received that to date. Please respond within 3
days to avoid having the item re-listed.
Thanks,
Lew
```

Q90 I just got paid! Now what do I do?

Prepare the package for shipment—that means taking every possible precaution to see that it arrives safely. Most eBay items can be shipped through the mail or via some other shipper, such as United Parcel Service or FedEx.

Once the item is shipped, here's a letter you might want to send to the high bidder:

```
Dear Bill:
I've sent out your package and would appreciate
it if you please let me know when it arrives.
I'd also appreciate it if you could leave some
feedback on eBay, which you may do via my eBay
homepage at http://members.ebay.com/aboutme/njs/.
I'll certainly reciprocate since your payment
arrived promptly which is much appreciated.
Thanks again, and I hope that you enjoy your
purchase.
Best wishes,
Lew
```

Once the package is out the door, the next thing you should do is leave some feedback (**Question 36**) about the buyer. As a rule, you should feel comfortable leaving a positive remark if the transaction went without incident. If you have a complaint, try to first settle it with the buyer so you can avoid leaving negative feedback. Negative feedback is a last resort used when no other means of mediating a dispute is effective.

Q91 Should I insure what I send?

Maybe. As of March 1, 1999, eBay is providing some coverage insurance for all transactions. It works something like this:

Any eBayer who does not have a negative feedback rating will have his or her transactions insured, and this insurance will be free until the six-month trial period for the program is over. Here are some of the guidelines and stipulations:

▶ The buyer and seller must have positive feedback ratings.

▶ The cost of the item being insured must be more than $25.00.

▶ Items can only be insured for up to $200.00. For additional insurance, contact the shipper (post office, FedEx, United Parcel Service, whoever is shipping the item).

▶ Items damaged during shipment are not covered. That is the responsibility of the shipper.

▶ There's a $25.00 deductible. If the final item bid was $48.00, insurance will pay you $23.00.

▶ You can only file one claim per month.

This insurance is a good idea, but it's not very comprehensive. Based on the particulars mentioned, items that are lost or damaged in transit are not covered. The only thing this insurance can help with is if the high bidder receives an item that she judges different from what was expected.

Insure the item through the service you used to deliver it. You can charge the bidder for this if you have explained that in your auction listing. Many sellers offer it as an option that the winning bidder can choose.

 **If I do have an insurance claim with eBay, how do I file it and when can I expect to get paid?**

Before you can submit a claim, you first have to file a complaint with the eBay Fraud Reporting System (**http://crs.ebay.com/frs/start.asp**). When such a complaint is filed, eBay makes an effort to contact the other party (be it a bidder or seller) and resolve the problem. Sometimes they are successful and sometimes they are not. If things really go sour (see the following sidebar), eBay will help you with information about how to contact law enforcement officials and what steps can then be taken.

Real Sour Grapes: A Lesson to Be Learned

Most eBayers are kind, courteous, and honest.
That's why it works so well. Then there are the
nightmares. Look at this unpleasant interaction
between an established and highly praised seller
and the high bidder. This is after the auction ended
for an item costing $2.00 and a shipping charge of
$3.50. As you can see, this interaction went
downhill fast:

Seller: *"I received your check today for the item you
bid on. However, the amount is incorrect. The
amount of the auction was $5.50 including postage;
you sent a check for $5.00. That doesn't cover the
postage. Please send the balance ASAP so we can
send your book."*

Buyer: *"I prefer that you send it 4th class—book
rate."*

Seller: *"We send via Priority or 1st class only. If you
had other wishes, you should have brought them
up sooner."*

Buyer: *"Are you sure this is the course of action you
wish? I am about to become hostile and
unreasonable."*

Seller: *"What are you talking about? We sent you an
email specifying the price and method of shipment.
You responded, agreed, and then sent an incorrect
payment. Now you imply that we are doing
something wrong? You agreed to the price of $5.50.
Are you retracting your payment? Please explain
what you are saying clearly enough (meaning more
than one-sentence emails) so we can try and
resolve this. Shipping costs are not postage. Packing
is an expense you will have to pay."*

Buyer: *"If you cash my check and I don't receive my
book via 4th class mail, I'll contact the FBI (mail
fraud), your local sheriff (misdemeanor theft) and the
IRS with the record of your sales I've just made from
the eBay.com records. I'll reserve the right to use
civil litigation to remedy any slander or recourse you
might attempt. It seems to me that it would be
easier for you to abide by the terms of the sale and
mail the book 4th class."*

Such disagreements are very difficult to resolve.
Better the buyer have a very clear understanding
(which this one obviously did not) about what's
expected. Perhaps it's even best to spell that out in
the "auction is over" letter you saw earlier.

 ## How can I be sure that the item I sent was received?

If you're sending really expensive items, you might also want
proof of delivery, regardless of the service that you are using.
This ensures that you know when the package has been
received and from who. Finally, several services now allow you
to track packages from the time they leave your hands to the
time they are delivered. You can do this via the telephone, but
it's much easier if you just go right to the service's Web site.
Here are some to consider:

▶ FedEx at **http://www.fedex.com/**

▶ United Parcel Service (UPS) at **http://www.ups/com/**

▶ Airborne at **http://www.airborne/com/**

▶ United States Postal Service at **http://www.usps.gov/**

I've had some great sales on eBay, but for the first time my items did not sell at my reserve price. What can I do now?

You are not entirely out of luck if an item doesn't sell. The first thing you should try to determine is why it didn't sell. Price too high? Auction too short? Item not sufficiently described? Placed in the wrong category?

How would you determine if it is any of these factors? The best thing is to look for other items on eBay that are similar to the one you put up. Find out what that has sold for (remember that you can look back at 30 days of auctions) or what the current bid is. See what category it's being offered in and remember that there are always new categories being added. Check the category overview (See **Question 9**).

More than 70% of eBay's offerings sell. If yours does not, you can re-list it under the following conditions:

▶ The reserve price that you specified was not met or exceeded. For example, you placed a reserve price of $20.00 on an item and you got one bid at $18.00.

▶ You got no bids.

Under these conditions, you can relist the item once more within 30 days of the previous auction's ending. If the item does sell, the insertion fee (at most, a whopping $2.00) is refunded. If the item still doesn't sell, you're out a maximum of $4.00 in insertion fees for the two listings.

Q95 How do I re-list an item?

To re-list an item, return to the completed Auction Item page and follow these steps:

1. Click on the link next to the Re-list Item area. When you do this, eBay shows you a short tutorial about how to make your item more attractive for sale.

2. Click the Re-list button, which is at the bottom of the page that contains the tips on selling.

3. Complete the Re-list Your Item form, the top of which you see in **Figure 3.13**. As you can see, the information from the original listing is already entered, so all you need do is modify what you think would increase the chances of the item selling.

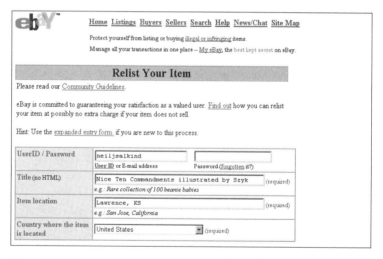

Figure 3.13 You are welcome to re-list an item if you did not sell it on the first try.

4. Click the Review button and review the information you provided. Click List when you are ready. You're back in business.

The Deadbeat Blues

These are the bidders who never make good on
their promise to pay. What a pain they can be. You
go to all kinds of efforts to offer them a good
product at a fair price and they renege. Not only is it
a disappointment and a waste of time for you, but it
means that all the other people who bid on this
item may indeed no longer be interested in bidding
again (since they think the item is gone and it might
be a lost cause).

What can you do? If you're sure that payment is not
forthcoming (in other words, your email messages
or another attempts to contact the high bidder go
unanswered), you can re-list the item, or contact the
next highest bidder and offer them the item at the
amount they bid.

There's not much more eBay fun than watching the bids on
your item go up and up and still up some more. Being a good
eBay seller can be part of a profitable business while you sell
those objects that people would otherwise have a very hard
time finding. By this point, you've learned eBay basics, how to
bid and buy and how to sell. All you need now is some time,
some neat item to list and a little bit of motivation to be on
your way as an eBay seller. Good luck, bid and sell smart, and
have fun.

Section 3 Selling

Appendix

Appendix

Appendix

Appendix

Appendix

Section 4
Appendix

Appendix

Appendix

ppendix

Appendix

pendix

Appendix A
Need Help?

This appendix doesn't discuss the kind of help that you get directly from eBay. This is the kind of help you get from programs that automatically bid for you and services that do everything but make your bank deposit for you (and they would probably do that as well if you asked).

Here's a brief overview of some of these services and offers. Know where the best place to find these is? Use the search tool on eBay and enter **ebay**. Strange, but true.

The Watcher

ISBN: 1-58490-007-5

Where to get it: http://www.scs-intl.com/

Price: $15.00 (with the Feedback Wizard: $25.00); mention this book and receive a 10% discount when you buy this software

What it does: The Watcher keeps an eye on your eBay activity, even when you can't. As you can see in the following figure, you enter your user ID whether you want to watch what you are selling or what you are bidding on, the interval to refresh the information, and to monitor current or closed auctions (just like eBay's search engine). The Watcher does the rest. It recovers the information in real time (refreshing at set intervals of 15 seconds to 10 minutes) and keeps you up-to-date regarding what is taking place with the items you are interested in. It will notify you of new bids, items you are the current high-bidder on, and items you aren't.

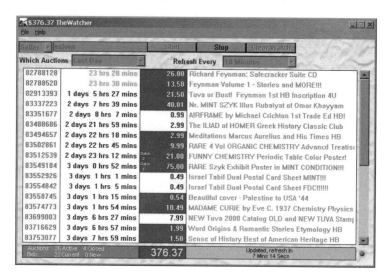

Section 4   Appendix A

The Feedback Wizard

ISBN: 1-58490-008-3

Where to get it: http://www.scs-intl.com/

Price: $15.00 (with The Watcher: $25.00); mention this book and receive a 10% discount when you buy this software

What it does: Just finished a bunch of selling and buying? Want to leave feedback for several different eBayers all at once? The Feedback Wizard allows you to leave feedback for several eBay sellers and bidders without having to wait for Web pages to load or having to find whom you want to leave feedback about. It's especially good for frequent eBay users, since you can do in minutes what would otherwise take hours.

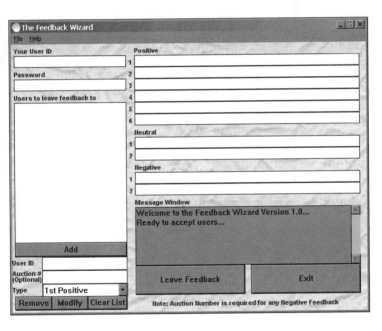

AuctionDesigner.com

Where to get it: http://www.AuctionDesigner.com

Price: $14.95 for lifetime membership; $24.95 for a lifetime membership with unlimited image hosting

What it does: This Web-based program makes it fast and easy to crate online ads, as well as lots of HTML templates. Among other things, here are some of the services that are provided:

▶ Unlimited image hosting for your auction items

▶ Predesigned HTML templates

▶ Technical support

▶ A referral plan that pays $5.00 cash for each person signed up

Section 5

Glossary

Glossary

Glossary

Glossary

Glossary

Glossary

Glossary

Want more information about a term listed in the glossary?
Go to the question that follows the definition.

ABOUT ME

A Web page stored on eBay that you can make to describe
yourself to other eBay users. Once you have created your own
About Me page, an icon appears next to your user ID.
See Question 56

ANNOUNCEMENTS BOARD

Where eBay posts information on changes regarding the way
things work and other announcements of general interest.
See Question 22

AOL CAFE

A special bulletin board where America Online users discuss any
topic they choose. *See Question 22*

BID CANCELLATION

When a seller cancels a bid. eBay suggests that this be done if
a seller is uncomfortable dealing with a particular bidder. *See*
bid retraction. *See Question 54*

Bid Increment

The minimum amount by which a bid can be raised. The increment increases as the amount of the highest bid increases. In some cases, if a proxy bid is made, the top bid may increase by less than the increment amount. See "Viewing the Confirmation" in "Selling" for the increments eBay follows. *See Question 64*

Bid Retraction

When a bidder cancels his own bid. The eBay Bid Retraction page explains more about this option, which should rarely be used. *See Question 54*

Bidder List

A list of items a user has bid on. The eBay Search page can create a customized list for you based on options you choose. *See Question 56*

Bidder Search

The search that results in a bidder list. See bidder list. *See Question 56*

Bidding

Offering to pay a specific amount for an item listed. The eBay FAQ page provides much valuable information on the bidding process. *See Question 43*

Big Ticket Items

Any item that receives a bid of $5,000.00 or more. These items are automatically listed on the eBay Big Ticket page.

Bulletin Boards

eBay pages where you can post and read messages. Boards are classified by topic and each category listing has its own. *See Question 22.* Here are some of these boards:

▶ Q&A Board

▶ The New Board

▶ The Wanted Board

▶ AOL Cafe

▶ eBay Cafe

▶ Holiday

▶ Emergency Contact

▶ International Trading

BUYER

The winning bidder of an auction. Also any bidder in an auction.

CATEGORY LISTING

A list of all the items on auction whose listings have indicated a particular category. Items are listed in the order they are submitted by sellers. The top item is always the most recent item listed. *See Question 9*

COMMISSION

eBay's payment when you sell an item at auction. It is in addition to the cost of placing a listing. *See Question 71*

COMPLETED SEARCH

A search by title of items on which bidding has completed. This option allows you to see what the going rate is for different types of items. It provides clues as to appropriate minimum bid amounts or reserve auction limits. The eBay Search page can create a Completed Search list for you. *See Question 29*

CONTACT INFORMATION

Your name, phone number, street address, and email address. eBay requires that all registered users provide this information. The information is used to resolve disputes and to ensure the community's integrity. Contact information can be given to other registered users if they request it, but only for eBay business.

Customer Support

eBay provides support for users in various ways. You can use email (**support@ebay.com**), the Frequently Asked Questions (FAQ) page, or the support bulletin boards. The site map answers many questions, as well. *See Question 23*

Discuss eBay's Newest Features

A bulletin board where you can do just what its name implies.

Dutch Auction

A format where the seller has more than one of the same item. Each bidder indicates how many he would like and the items are then sold to all bidders at the lowest acceptable bid price. Typically, the seller sets a minimum bid at which she is willing to sell the items. The competition for the bidders is not only for the best price, but for as many of the item as they want. *See Question 54*

eBay Store

Where you can order eBay logo-embossed clothes, hats, and other items.

FAQ

Frequently Asked Questions. These are the most often asked, and the most important questions that new and experienced eBay users can ask. The FAQ's are found on the site map under Information.

Featured Auction

A listing of items for which the sellers have paid an extra fee to get extra exposure. Sellers must have a feedback rating of 10 or more for the privilege. Each category listing area has featured auction items appearing at the top of the listing, and there is also a grand featured auction area, which presents items from all categories. *See Question 67*

FEEDBACK

Your permanent record. Buyers and sellers can post information—positive, negative, or neutral—about transactions. Feedback can make or break an eBay citizen's reputation. You get points for positive feedback and lose points for negative feedback. Stars appear next to users who have built up positive feedback. *See Question 33*

FINAL VALUE FEE

A fee that sellers pay to eBay when an item sells. The amount of the fee is based on the final selling price, or *final value*, of the item. You pay a lot if you sell a really expensive item; you pay just a tiny amount if you sell a really inexpensive item. This fee, along with the insertion fee, is how the eBay community supports itself financially and can afford to repave all those Internet highways. Buyers never pay a fee. *See Question 71*

GIFT ICON

A seasonally appropriate icon (a heart for Valentine's day, or an Easter Egg for Easter, etc.) that tells you that the sellers think this item would make a nice gift. There is a Gift Section at eBay, along with their regular category listing. The seller paid a small fee for the special treatment.

GIVING BOARD

A posting area where you can share or learn of charitable opportunities you can offer.

GOT A QUESTION?

A search page that locates eBay Help pages covering your topic of interest. You can access this page through the Help Desk. *See Question 23*

HELP DESK

An eBay page with links to support and answers to a variety of questions. *See Question 23*

Section 5 Glossary

HOME

The main eBay page. From here, you can go anywhere and do anything on eBay. *See Question 4*

HOT ITEMS

Any item with more than 30 bids. There is a special listing of hot items, as well as an icon that appears next to the item listing in their regular location. A reserve auction price item is ineligible as a hot item. *See Question 26*

HTML

The computer code (Hypertext Markup Language) that displays pages on the Web. Also used to format pages that can enhance your item listing with colors, pictures, and links to your auction. *See Question 80*

INSERTION FEE

The cost of putting an item up for auction on eBay. The fee is charged when an item listing is submitted and is based on the minimum bid value or the reserve price, whichever is higher. One of two fees sellers are asked to pay. *See Question 71*

ITEM LOOKUP

A search function that finds the full listing for any item number. It can be accessed from the Search page, as well as other areas.

ITEM NUMBER

The official identification number assigned by eBay to each and every item put up for auction. It allows tracking the progress and results of different auctions, even when the descriptions of the items are similar. It is useful to include this number in all email transactions between sellers and buyers so that there is no doubt which item is being discussed.

LISTING

An organized grouping of items and auctions matching some search criteria; the description of an item and its auction; the item up for auction. *See Question 29*

LURKERS

eBayers who hang around, checking out eBay, browsing, and asking questions. Lurking is acceptable and encouraged on eBay! *See Question 25*

MAXIMUM BID

The most a bidder is willing to pay for an item. This is information the bidder provides to eBay when the proxy bidding method is used. It is also useful for all bidders to have this figure in mind, even if they are bidding on their own. *See Question 46*

MINIMUM BID

The lowest bid a seller is willing to accept for an item. This amount becomes the lowest beginning bid that can be accepted by the system. It must be at least one penny. *See reserve auction. See Question 46*

MY EBAY

A one-stop personalized well of information about you and your present standing as a bidder, seller, or all-around eBay citizen. This page provides current bids on auctions you are involved in, recent feedback, and a sampling of listings from your favorite categories. A word of caution—do not ever send the link to your "My eBay" page to any other user. It contains you password (encoded) and can give away important information like your maximum bids. *See Question 56*

NEW

Items that appeared in the last 24 hours. An eBay-generated icon appears next to new listings.

NEWBIES

Friendly term used by old eBayers for new eBayers.

NEWS/ANNOUNCEMENTS

An eBay location where you will find all the latest information. *See Question 24*

NEWS/CHAT

An eBay page that provides links to bulletin boards, support options, and chat areas. *See Question 24*

OUTBID

When someone else proves that they are willing to pay more for an item than you are.

PIC

An eBay-generated icon which means a picture has been attached to an item listing. eBay knows a graphic has been attached because a URL has been entered during the item listing process. *See Question 83*

PRIVATE AUCTIONS

Auctions in which the email addresses of seller and bidder are not shown. An option chosen by the seller if the item will attract bids by people who may not want their identity known. Rarely used, and then usually for Big Ticket Items or less expensive, but more embarrassing items. *See Question 54*

PROXY BIDDING

An amazingly useful feature where a bidder enters the maximum amount he is willing to pay. For the remainder of the auction, eBay acts as his representative and continues to bid as necessary until the auction either ends or you are outbid. It may sound risky to trust someone (or something, in this case) else to bid for you, but the eBay computers can do simple math and will only increase your bid the minimum amount required by the bidding rules. eBay will never bid more than you have authorized. It is proxy bidding that results in the sometimes frustrating experience of entering a bid and immediately being told you have been outbid. *See Question 47*

Q&A BOARD

A posting location where eBay users ask and answer each others' questions. *See Question 23*

REGISTERED USER

To buy or sell you must be registered on eBay. Registration is free and helps to keep eBay the happy, pollution-free town it is. *See Question 14*

REGISTRATION

A one-time process of introducing yourself to eBay and establishing that you are who you claim to be.
See Question 14

RELISTING

If an item hasn't sold at the end of an auction, the seller has the option to relist it within 30 days without having to re-type the descriptive information. eBay's current pricing structure makes relisting an appealing option since if the item sells, you get the relisting fee back. *See Question 95*

RESERVE PRICE

The lowest winning bid a seller is willing to accept. This is different than the minimum bid, as the reserve is not revealed to bidders. An example may explain the distinction: You wish to sell your prized Grand Canyon painted ceramic thimble. You think it's worth $50.00, but you are willing to sell it for $25.00. You would like some rock 'em, sock 'em bidding action on this item, so you set a low minimum bid of $1.00 just to get the auction rolling. You have set a reserve price of $25.00, though. If the final bid does not reach $25.00, you are not obligated to sell. Buyers are told that your auction is a reserve auction, but will not be told the reserve price. Some bidders don't like

Section 5 Glossary

reserve auctions because they never know how far away they are from the reserve. Once someone's bid has reached the reserve price, however, the listing indicates as much. If you are participating via proxy bidding, your bid is increased immediately to the reserve price if it is at or lower than your maximum bid. *See Question 53*

SafeHarbor

eBay's community watchdog organization. This is the place to turn for complaints about other citizens. Write them at **safeharbor@ebay.com**.

Search

A service available on many eBay pages. Enter keywords; eBay searches through its massive collection of items for current auctions that might interest you. Searching allows you to sort results in many useful ways. *See Question 29*

Secure Server

A safe computer setup that allows you to send eBay your credit card number in a way that prevents bad guys from getting access to it. Look for the "key" or "lock" icon in your browser status bar to be sure a secure server is being used.

Seller

The eBay user who offers an item at auction.

Seller List

A list accessible through the Search page, it displays information on all the current auctions for any particular seller. You can keep track of your own auctions this way; you can also see the listings for another seller.

Shades

An icon indicating that the registered user has changed her user ID in the last 30 days. *See Question 18*

SHILLING

Bidding on one's own item (often using a second or third account which often uses a free email service such as Yahoo! or HotMail) to increase the bid. This is absolutely forbidden at eBay. A seller can control the selling price of an item through the use of minimum bids and reserves, so other than just plain nastiness, there's no reason for a seller to consider this practice.

SIPHONING

Soliciting bidders from another sellers' auction to bid on your auction. This is against eBay's rules.

SITE MAP

The mother of all eBay pages. Every link imaginable for every eBay activity can be found here. This is the only way to find your way to certain pages. *See Question 19*

SNIPING

Winning an item by placing the winning bid at that very last second, especially if that is the sniper's very first bid in the auction. It is frustrating to be on the losing end of a successful sniper, but there is nothing wrong with the practice. *See* maximum bid and proxy bidding for ways to avoid feeling victimized.

SPAM

Also known as junk mail. Some sellers offer items only to solicit names of interested parties to get their email addresses for mailing lists. If you bid on an item (perhaps MS Office 97 Pro) and suddenly start getting emails from sellers offering it to you for less, you have been the victim of this ruse. These sellers prefer to handle transactions offline in order to avoid paying eBay's fees.

Starting Price

The first and lowest bid that will be accepted at the auction. It is the minimum bid price the seller has chosen.

Title Search

A search of current items that matches keywords to the item's title. Searches can also look for the keywords in the item description. *See Question 29*

URL

Internet-speak for the World Wide Web address, or location, of a specific Web page or graphic; **http://www.ebay.com** is an example. When including a picture with your item listing, you must place the picture on the Web and indicate its URL.

User Agreement

The list of rules and legal protections established by you and eBay before you become a registered user. You'll have an opportunity to read this ponderous document during the registration process. *See Question 7*

User ID

A name you decide upon for your online nickname. If you don't choose a name, your email address automatically becomes your user ID. You can change this ID only once every 30 days. *See Question 14*

Wanted Board

A bulletin board on which you can list all those things you really want to buy, but never seem to see offered at auction. *See Question 31*

Section 6

Index

Index

Index

Section VI   Index

N

O

P

Q

R

S

CREATING
PAINT SHOP PRO
WEB GRAPHICS

Price: $44.99
ISBN: 0-9662889-0-4
Pages: 384
Author: Andy Shafran

- Full Color

- Foreword by
  Chris Anderson,
  VP of Marketing,
  Jasc Software

Highlights:

- Sixteen focused chapters that teach
  you how to understand layers, special
  effects, plug-ins, and other important Paint
  Shop Pro features

- Integrates with a comprehensive Website that
  contains updated information, complete
  examples, and frequently asked questions

- Detailed Web specific topics such as
  transparency, animation, web art, digital
  photography, scanners, and more

MUSKA & LIPMAN

MP3 POWER!
WITH
WINAMP

Price: $29.99
ISBN: 0-9662889-3-9
Pages: 320
Authors: Justin Frankel,
         Ben Sawyer,
         Dave Greely

• CD-ROM with
  software, utilities,
  and popular music

Highlights:

• Unique and complete coverage of
  MP3 technology and Winamp technical
  specifications and optimizations. Ideal for
  casual and expert MP3 users

• Covers creating MP3 files from existing CDs,
  finding MP3 files on the Internet, and
  marketing MP3 files for others to download
  and use

• Discusses finding and building virtual radio
  stations on the Internet

MUSKA&LIPMAN

QuicKeys
Solutions for
Windows and Mac

Price: $24.99
ISBN: 0-9662889-5-5
Pages: 240
Author: Don Crabb

- Solution-focused
  format
- CD-ROM with
  valuable
  software
- Includes $20
  coupon towards
  QuicKeys software

Highlights:

- Teaches you how to get around shortcomings
  in Windows and Mac OS using QuicKeys
  to automate repetitive and complicated
  procedures
- Shows how to turn common or complex sets
  of commands into a single keystroke, saving
  you significant time
- Comfortable book tone for novice and
  power users

MUSKA & LIPMAN

CREATING GEOCITIES WEBSITES

Price: $39.99
ISBN: 0-9662889-1-2
Pages: 352
Authors: Ben Sawyer,
           Dave Greely

- Full-color
- Foreword by
  David Bohnnett
  & John Rezner,
  co-founders of
  GeoCities

Highlights:

- Complete coverage of the free Geocities
  tools, services, and programs
- Developed in conjunction with GeoCities'
  technical staff
- Full color guide with dozens of templates,
  tricks, and techniques

MUSKA & LIPMAN

MUSKA&LIPMAN

Order Form

Postal Orders:
Muska & Lipman Publishing
9525 Kenwood Road, Suite 16-372
Cincinnati, Ohio 45242

On-Line Orders or more information:
http://www.muskalipman.com
Fax Orders:
(513) 794-1913

Qty.	Title	ISBN	Price	Total Cost
_____	*Creating Paint Shop Pro Web Graphics*	0-9662889-0-4	$44.99	_____
_____	*Creating GeoCities Websites*	0-9662889-1-2	$39.99	_____
_____	*eBay Online Auctions*	0-9662889-4-7	$14.99	_____
_____	*MP3 Power! with Winamp*	0-9662889-3-9	$29.99	_____
_____	*QuicKeys Solutions for Windows and Mac*	0-9662889-5-5	$24.99	_____

Subtotal	_____
Sales Tax (please add 6% for books shipped to Ohio addresses)	_____
Shipping ($4.00 for the first book, $2.00 each additional book)	_____
TOTAL PAYMENT ENCLOSED	_____

Ship to:

Company _____

Name _____

Address _____

City _____

State _____ Zip _____ Country _____

Educational facilities, companies, and organizations interested in multiple copies of these books should contact the publisher for quantity discount information. Training manuals, CD-ROMs, electronic versions, and portions of these books are also available individually or can be tailored for specific needs.

Thank you for your order.